Amazing Facts in Science

By
DON BLATTNER

COPYRIGHT © 2007 Mark Twain Media, Inc.

ISBN 978-1-58037-427-9

Printing No. CD-404076

Mark Twain Media, Inc., Publishers
Distributed by Carson-Dellosa Publishing Company, Inc.

Table of Contents

Table of Contents (cont.)

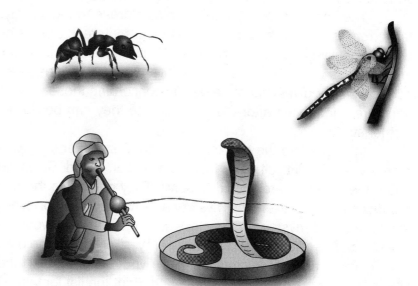

Introduction

Students love to learn about science. They are especially fond of discovering interesting, bizarre, and often surprising scientific facts. These unusual facts that students enjoy are often considered unimportant and ignored in lesson plans. Here are a few examples:

- The United States Defense Department studied spider webs in order to see if they are strong enough to be used in bulletproof vests.
- When a male mudskipper fish wants a mate, it does push-ups.
- An African lungfish can survive out of water for four years.
- Clownfish are unusual in that they are able to change their sex.
- Police have been known to use snapping turtles to help them find dead human bodies.
- Pufferfish, which contain a nerve poison that is 10,000 times more deadly than cyanide, is used as food in Japan.
- Cephalopods, which include octopuses and cuttlefish, communicate by changing colors.
- Some land snails court by shooting darts at each other.
- Whenever a sea cucumber encounters an enemy, it spits out its intestines.
- In colonial times, lobsters were fed only to slaves.
- The tailorbird was given its name because it sews.
- There is a bird that can imitate chain saws, barking dogs, and cars.
- Some birds use ants as an insect repellent.
- The saber-toothed blenny fish gets some of its meals by pretending to be a maid.
- The Goliath frog of West Africa is two and half feet long.
- The Food and Drug Administration will allow an average of 400 or more insect fragments or an average of 11 or more rodent hairs per 50 grams of ground cinnamon.
- Ants, termites, and bark beetles were all farmers before humans were.
- When a male deathwatch beetle is ready to mate, it attracts a female by banging its head against a wall.

This book is designed as a series of quizzes that includes these, and many other, amazing facts about science. It doesn't deal with all of the important facts about science that students learn in school. Instead, by revealing little-known scientific facts, students are encouraged to learn more.

The book is especially valuable as a pre-learning activity. Prior to studying a unit, one of the tests from this book should pique a student's interest, arouse his or her curiosity, and give a different perspective to what he or she is about to learn. It will be a springboard for discussion. Just as important as the facts and answers, are the explanations after each quiz. The explanation of the correct answer gives elaborate details concerning these unusual facts. The answers and explanations are printed just after the questions so they can be duplicated and given to the students for further study.

In addition to the quizzes, there are puzzles and logic problems. Some are very easy, and others are quite difficult. Also, there is a section called "Scientific Mysteries." These are actual mysteries the students are invited to solve. They can solve the mystery by themselves, in groups, or the teacher may present the mystery as a twenty-question type of activity. In this case, the teacher would read the mystery to the class, and the students would try to solve it by asking the teacher questions. The teacher can only answer "yes" or "no" to the questions.

Here's another suggestion. Have your students start their own list of strange and unusual scientific facts they find in their research. Print the list for your students at the end of the year.

Name: _____ Date: _____

Science Trivia: True or False?

Directions: Indicate if the statements listed below are "True" or "False" by circling the correct response.

True   False   1. Until the early 1960s, silk threads were used in gun sights.

True   False   2. Spiders are among the oldest insects.

True   False   3. A sea lion will get seasick if put onboard a ship.

True   False   4. The wood frog doesn't croak like many frogs, but quacks like a duck.

True   False   5. A geoduck is a duck in Europe.

True   False   6. Only the female canary sings.

True   False   7. The total weight of insects eaten by spiders every year is more than the combined weight of the entire human population.

True   False   8. By weight, spider silk is twice as strong as steel.

True   False   9. More human deaths have been caused by fleas than by all of the wars ever fought.

True   False   10. The desert locust (*Schistocera gregaria*), which inhabits India, Africa, and the Middle East, may be the most destructive insect in the world.

True   False   11. The Neanderthal's brain was smaller than yours.

True   False   12. To defend the colony, some termites shoot glue from a gun on their heads.

True   False   13. Mars is called the "red planet" because it is rusty.

True   False   14. Queen termites may live for fifty years.

True   False   15. A tarantula is able to go one year without eating.

True   False   16. A female sea horse stores her babies inside her stomach.

True   False   17. A giant squid's eyes are smaller than that of a goldfish.

True   False   18. The jellyfish is not a single animal, but a colony of animals.

True   False   19. If a person has part of his or her liver removed because of an accident or to be used in a transplant, it will grow back in a few months.

True   False   20. A rainbow is a colored arc in the sky.

True   False   21. The sound one hears when someone cracks his or her knuckles is caused by ligaments snapping.

True   False   22. One of the main ingredients in glass is sand.

True   False   23. Whenever human plasma, the liquid part of blood or lymph, is not available, coconut water is sometimes substituted.

True   False   24. Natural gas has an odor that smells like rotten eggs.

True   False   25. Without gravity, astronauts get taller.

True   False   26. The funny bone is a bone in the elbow.

True   False   27. The Food and Drug Administration has a rule that brined, fresh, canned, or frozen maraschino cherries cannot contain an average of 5% or more cherry pieces that were rejected due to maggots.

True   False   28. If a sponge is cut into pieces and squeezed through a screen so that it is just a bunch of loose cells, it will reassemble itself into a completely functioning organism.

True   False   29. Sharks can sense a drop of blood from ten miles away.

1

Name: _____ Date: _____

Which Was Invented First?

Directions: Look at the two pairs of inventions shown below. On the line next to each pair, write which you think was invented first.

1. Toothbrush or toothpaste? _____

2. Airplane or parachute? _____

3. Mechanical reaper or crop insurance? _____

4. Pendulum clock or pocket watch? _____

5. Beer or soap? _____

6. Traffic lights or automobiles? _____

7. Automobiles or odometers? (An odometer is the device on the dashboard of a car that measures the total number of miles traveled.) _____

8. Medical textbook or paper? _____

9. Eyeglasses or false teeth? _____

10. Plywood or glass? _____

11. Bread-slicing machine or pop-up toaster? _____

12. Dynamite or bombs? _____

13. Elevator or skyscraper? _____

14. Automatic calculator or adding machine? _____

15. Telephone answering machine or talking movies? _____

16. Remote control or television set? _____

17. Gasoline-powered automobile or steam-powered automobile? _____

18. Sunglasses or eyeglasses? _____

19. Washing machine or dishwasher? _____

20. Golf or tennis? _____

21. Bifocals or blue jeans? _____

22. Match or cigarette lighter? _____

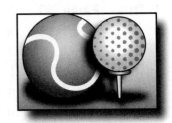

Which Was Invented First?—Answers

1. **Toothpaste**. When we think of toothpaste, we think of it as being used with a toothbrush. However, toothpaste was actually invented about 1,200 years before the toothbrush. The first known toothpaste was used in fourth-century Egypt. It was a compound made of salt, pepper, mint, and flowers. Several centuries later, the Romans used toothpaste that included human urine. Apparently, the ammonia in the urine whitened the teeth. Before the invention of the toothbrush, ancient people cleaned their teeth with twigs and wood. As people became more civilized, they would rub chalk or baking soda on their teeth with cloth or rags. It wasn't until 1498 that the first toothbrush was made for the emperor of China. It consisted of a bone handle with hog bristles. Toothbrushes did not come into general use in the West until the seventeenth century.

2. **Parachute**. A few medieval documents record the use of parachute-like devices to allow a person to fall (somewhat) safely from a certain height. In A.D. 852, a Muslim named Armen Firman jumped from a tower in Cordoba using a crude parachute. He sustained a few injuries. Three hundred years later, another Muslim tried to duplicate this feat in Constantinople, but was hurt so badly that he eventually died of his injuries. The first really successful parachute was invented by Sebastien Lenormand in 1783. He was the one who first called it a "parachute." Two years later, Jean-Pierre Blanchard demonstrated a parachute by throwing a dog attached to a parachute out of a hot air balloon. He later used a parachute to jump out of a balloon himself. While there were gliders before the Wright brothers' flight, Orville and Wilbur Wright are recognized for building and testing the first powered airplane. The test flight of their airplane took place at Kitty Hawk, North Carolina, on December 17, 1903.

3. **Crop insurance**. Cyrus Hall McCormick was an American farmer and inventor who invented the mechanical reaper in 1831. Benjamin Franklin was an author, scientist, printer, diplomat, and inventor. Franklin suggested crop insurance about a century before McCormick invented the reaper.

4. **Pocket watch**. Early civilizations began marking time by seasons. It is estimated that, about 6,000 years ago, some civilizations began to create devices to divide the day into segments. They first made devices that used the sun to mark time. Water clocks were used by Egyptians, Greeks, and other civilizations. These were stone pots that had sloping sides, enabling the water to drip out at a constant rate, or metal bowls with a hole in the bottom. Later, water clocks became more sophisticated. Mechanical clocks appeared in Italy in the fourteenth century. In 1510, Peter Henlein of Nuremberg invented a watch that could be carried. It was the forerunner of the modern pocket watch. Christiaan Huygens, a well-known Dutch mathematician and physicist, was interested in making accurate clocks for navigation. In 1657, he invented the pendulum clock.

5. **Beer**. Beer is one of the oldest beverages made by humans. Many different civilizations made beer using any kind of food that contained specific kinds of sugars capable of fermentation. There is evidence that beer was used as far back as 5,000 B.C. in the country now known as Iran. The earliest known formula for soap was used in Babylonia in 2200 B.C. It consisted of alkali, water, and an oil that gave the soap a scent like cinnamon. Ancient Egyptians bathed with a soap made from alkaline salts and the oils of animals and vegetables.

Which Was Invented First?—Answers (cont.)

6. **Traffic lights.** There were a few mechanical vehicles prior to 1885, but many believe that the German, Karl Benz, made the first real automobile in 1885. Before automobiles, there were horses and buggies, and traffic was such a problem that police officers had to direct traffic. The world's first traffic signal was installed in London in 1868. It was a revolving gas-powered lantern with green and red signals. Green meant "caution," and red meant "stop." It was turned by a police officer.

7. **Odometer.** It is thought that Archimedes may have invented the first odometer. It was later described by a Roman writer in 23 B.C. Every revolution of the wheel of the chariot engaged a 400-tooth cogwheel, which in turn engaged another gear that dropped a pebble into a box. Every 400 rotations equaled a Roman mile, which was about 1,400 meters. A wheel turn was 1/400 of a mile. All a person needed to do was count the pebbles to find out how far a chariot had traveled. Another version of the odometer was invented in ancient China by Zhang Heng. Karl Benz made the first real automobile powered by an internal-combustion engine in 1885.

8. **Medical textbook.** Written communication was a major leap forward for a civilization. About 4000 B.C., the Sumerians wrote on clay. While clay worked for a writing surface, it was not practical. For many centuries, people tried to find better surfaces upon which to write. Silk, bamboo, cloth, and wood are just some of the materials tried as a writing surface. Egyptians processed papyrus, a plant available along the Nile River, as a writing surface. The word "paper" is taken from the word "papyrus," but papyrus was not really considered paper. Ts'ai Lun of China is the one generally credited with inventing paper in the year A.D. 105. Using the bark of a mulberry tree and bamboo fibers, he mixed them with water, pounded them, and poured the resulting mixture onto a flat piece of coarsely woven cloth. The water drained through and left the fibers on the cloth. The resulting paper was lightweight, cheap, and easy to make. It would take more than a thousand years for this process to make its way to Europe. Early medical textbooks were not written on paper. The civilizations between the Tigris and Euphrates Rivers, the area that is now called the Middle East, thrived from 3000 B.C. These people wrote on clay and other materials. There are forty clay tablets, dating from about 700 B.C. that give diagnoses and cures for various diseases. It is called *The Treatise of Medical Diagnoses and Prognoses*. Ancient Egyptians recorded accounts of the medical practices available in 2,000 B.C., which included case studies and remedies. There are other records on papyrus that date back to 1600 B.C. and 1550 B.C. The Greeks wrote down medical practices around 500 B.C.

9. **False teeth.** Although we don't know for sure when eyeglasses were invented, it is likely they were invented in northern Italy in the late 1280s. Who invented them is unknown, although Arabs had magnifying lenses in the tenth century, so there is speculation that they might have been involved. China invented eyeglasses at about the same time. The first spectacles were held by hand and later just put on the bridge of the nose. They were later held with a ribbon over a person's head, and then held in place by a hat. It wasn't until 1727 that a British optician developed glasses that were held in place by earpieces fitting over the ears. False teeth, also called dentures, were made of bone and ivory and were in use by 700 B.C. In the eighteenth century, false teeth were carved by hand and held in place by silk threads. They were so crude at this time that people had to take them out of their mouths in order to eat. Later, false teeth were held in place with steel springs.

4

Which Was Invented First?—Answers (cont.)

10. **Plywood.** Glass occurs naturally in nature. Obsidian, which is produced from volcanoes, is an example. However, the first record of glass being made by humans occurred in about 1500 B.C. in Egypt. Glass-blowing was developed in the first century.

    Plywood is made up of thin sheets of wood that are stacked together. The grain of each sheet of wood is stacked at a 90-degree-angle from the last layer. The layers are glued together under pressure and heat. Plywood was used in Ancient Egypt around 3500 B.C. Since there was a shortage of good wood in Egypt, a high quality of wood was glued over a poor quality of wood to give the impression that the entire piece of wood was made of the higher-quality wood.

11. **Pop-up toaster.** Bread is one of the first prepared foods that humans created. It consisted of cereal grains mixed with water, making a paste, and then it was cooked. General Electric patented the first electric toaster in 1909, although Hotpoint says that they had made a toaster prior to the one produced by GE. These first toasters required the user to constantly watch the toaster and take out the toast before it burned. The pop-up toaster, which actually ejects the toast when it is ready, was invented by Charles Strite in 1919.

    While people tore or sliced bread over the years, it wasn't until 1928 that Otto Frederick Rohwedder developed a machine to slice and wrap bread. His first invention was a machine that only sliced the bread. It was not widely used because bakers were afraid that sliced bread would dry out.

12. **Bombs.** There is some evidence that gunpowder was probably invented in China about A.D. 850. It was not originally used for military purposes. In the eleventh century in China, bombs made of gunpowder were fired from catapults. The Chinese also developed "firing cannons," which were tubes of bamboo filled with gunpowder that would throw a flaming missile at the enemy. The first gun with a metal barrel was in use by A.D. 1290. Today, gunpowder is used mainly in fireworks. Dynamite, which is an explosive made from nitroglycerin and other materials, was discovered by Alfred B. Nobel, a Swedish chemist, in 1866. He also established the Nobel Prizes in his will. First awarded in 1901, the prizes have become very distinguished awards.

13. **Elevator.** Primitive hoists and elevators were in use as early as the third century B.C. They were operated by humans, animals, or waterwheels. In the nineteenth century, power elevators, mostly steam-operated, were widely used in factories and mines. Elisha Otis is a name that it is often associated with elevators. Strangely enough, Otis did not invent an elevator. What he invented in 1852 was a brake that is used in modern elevators. The brake made elevators safer and paved the way for skyscrapers. Work began on what is considered the first skyscraper in 1884 in Chicago. It used a steel-framed interior and was nine stories high. In 1891, two more stories were added. In 1931, the building was demolished.

14. **Automatic calculator.** A computing device was invented in Babylonia about 5,000 years ago. It was called an **abacus**. The abacus was a frame made of wood that had a series of beads that could be slid up or down. It enabled a person to add, subtract, multiply, and divide. A person who knows how to operate an abacus can calculate as quickly as someone using a modern electronic calculator. However, the abacus was not a mechanical calculator. The person who received credit for inventing the first automatic calculator was Wilhelm Schickard, a minister and a professor in Germany, in 1623. This device was called the calculating clock and could add and subtract six-figure numbers. Only two calculating

5

Which Was Invented First?—Answers (cont.)

clocks were produced, and they did not have a program stored inside them. The adding machine was invented in 1642 by a nineteen-year-old French boy named Blaise Pascal. His father was a clerk and needed to make a large number of math calculations every day, so Blaise invented a simple machine that was capable of adding and subtracting very quickly.

15. **Telephone answering machine.** Valdemar Poulsen, a Danish telephone engineer and inventor, invented the Telegraphone in 1898. It was the first practical device for recording and reproducing sound. The Telegraphone recorded sound on a wire and was used to record telephone conversations. Films, or movies, as they are often called, were originally silent with the actors conveying the meaning of the film by their actions or with dialogue flashed at the bottom of the screen. Early attempts to add sound to films encountered a major problem. The sound device was separate from the film, and the two would often not be synchronized. In other words, an actor's lips would begin to move, and then a short time later, the audience would hear what he or she was saying. In 1923, Lee DeForest overcame this problem when he invented the first film where the sound was actually recorded on the side of the film, so it was impossible for it not to be synchronized with the images on the screen. He made several films using this process. The most famous of the early talking movies was *The Jazz Singer* in 1927.

16. **Remote control.** Nikola Tesla was a Croatian-born American physicist, electrical engineer, and inventor. He was a pioneer in the use of alternating current electricity and invented the alternating current induction generator, which changed mechanical energy into alternating current electricity. In 1898, Tesla demonstrated a remote control by guiding two model boats on the lake in Madison Square Garden in New York City. Remote devices have been used to control cars, boats, planes, television sets, and other devices. Philo Taylor Farnsworth was an American who conceived the idea for the vacuum tube television display, developing it when he was only 21 years old. Farnsworth's other television patents covered focusing, power, scanning, synchronizing, contrast, controls, and power. The first patents for the Farnsworth television system were filed January 1927. Many people considered this the official date of the invention of television.

17. **Gasoline-powered automobile.** Karl Benz made the first real automobile powered by an internal-combustion engine in 1885. Sylvester Howard Roper was an American inventor who developed the first steam-driven car in 1889.

18. **Sunglasses.** Eyeglasses were likely invented in northern Italy in the late 1280s, but devices to protect a person's eyes from the sun were invented by several ancient civilizations. Archaeologists have uncovered evidence that sunglasses may have been invented even before writing was invented. Early natives of what is now Alaska made sunglasses of ivory. Ancient Africans used bones to protect their eyes. It is believed that the tinting of glasses began in 1300 when Chinese judges wore smoke-colored, tinted quartz lenses in order to hide their eye expressions in court. About 1,430 vision-correcting, smoke-colored lenses were in use at that time.

19. **Dishwasher.** Josephine Cochrane, who lived in Shelbyville, Illinois, invented the dishwasher in 1886. Mrs. Cochrane was a rich woman, and although she had servants who did the dishes, she was always annoyed when a servant broke a dish. Also, she thought it just took too long to wash the dishes, since she had many large dinner parties. So she took

Which Was Invented First?—Answers (cont.)

a copper boiler and designed wire compartments into which the different kinds of dishes fit. The compartments were placed on a wheel that lay flat inside the boiler. When the motor was turned on, the wheel turned, and hot, soapy water shot up from the bottom. Her invention was so successful that many who saw it asked her to make one for them. She eventually patented the design of this machine.

When humans first began wearing clothes, they scrubbed them on stones in streams and rivers. This worked for many centuries, but eventually people made washboards to replace stones, and the streams were replaced by tubs. The first electric, motorized washer was invented by Alva Fisher in 1907.

20. **Tennis**. Many early civilizations, such as the ancient Egyptians, Greeks, and Romans, played games in which a ball was batted or hit, but these games were much different than the modern game of tennis. Most historians say the modern game of tennis can be traced back to the eleventh or twelfth centuries. French monks played a game where they hit a handball against the monastery walls or over a rope stretched across a courtyard. Eventually, a glove was put on the bare hand, later a paddle was used, and finally a racquet was designed. The ball, which had begun as a wad of wool or hair, took on several changes, and the wall was replaced by a net. Others took up the game, and it became so popular that Louis IV and the Pope tried to ban the game of tennis.

While some argue where and when the game of golf began, most agree that the game had its beginnings in Scotland. The original game was different than it is today, but it did involve a crude kind of club and the movement of a ball from one place to another using as few strokes as possible. The first reference to golf occurred in 1457 when King James II of Scotland issued a ban on the playing of both golf and soccer. The king felt his archers were spending so much time on these games that they weren't practicing their archery.

21. **Bifocals**. Benjamin Franklin had two pairs of glasses. One pair enabled him to focus on things close to him, and another enabled him to focus on things farther away. He became frustrated every time he had to change his glasses when he needed to focus at a different distance. So in 1784, he had the lenses of two pairs of his glasses cut in two and put half of each lens in one frame. These were the first bifocal glasses.

Levi Strauss, an immigrant from Bavaria, was selling tents and wagon covers made of canvas in the California goldfields. When a man asked him what he was selling, Strauss told him. The man said he really needed some pants that would withstand rough treatment. In 1850, Strauss decided to make some pants out of the canvas. The men liked the pants, but said they were too rough, so Strauss substituted a twilled cotton cloth from France, which later became known as denim.

22. **Cigarette lighter.** In 1816, a German chemist named J.W. Dobereiner invented a way of automatically igniting a jet of hydrogen, which he called "Dobereiner's Lamp." While its purpose was not to light cigarettes, it was a mechanical means of creating a flame, and the idea was later used to create devices specifically to light cigarettes. In 1827, John Walker, an English chemist and apothecary, invented the first match. He coated the end of a stick with certain chemicals. After the stick dried, it could be rubbed against a surface, causing it to ignite. This was the first friction match.

Name: _____ Date: _____

The Name Is the Same

Directions: Chances are that you have never heard the word "eponym." Eponym refers to a person whose name is the source of an invention, process, city, or even era. For example, the "Bessemer process," which is an inexpensive industrial process for the mass-production of steel from molten pig iron, was named after its inventor, Henry **Bessemer**. Various inventions are described below. You are to fill in the blank with the name of the person associated with the invention or the name of the invention itself. Sometimes the invention is spelled differently than that of the name of the person after whom the invention is named.

1. While he did not invent this knife, this famous adventurer was a hero of early Texas. His name was Jim _____.

2. The French inventor of this system of writing and printing for the blind was named Louis _____.

3. This wrench has a jaw that can be adjusted in order for it to turn different sizes of nuts. It was invented by a London blacksmith named Charles Moncke. _____

4. This brush for artists is made from an animal's hair. It was invented by a Frenchman whose last name was _____.

5. The world's best-selling doll was first sold in 1959. It was named after the creator's daughter. This doll's name is _____.

6. Hans _____, along with Walther Muller, developed an instrument that detects and measures the intensity of radiation.

7. While Joseph-Ignace _____ of France did not invent this mechanical device used to execute people by decapitation (cutting off their heads), his name is associated with the machine.

8. George _____, Jr., invented this amusement park ride, which consisted of a large wheel that rotated on a shaft. There were a number of seats on the wheel that carried passengers.

9. This weapon is a machine gun that has several barrels revolving around a central axis and can be fired quickly. The weapon was first used in the Civil War. The gun is named for its inventor, Richard Jordan _____, a physician.

10. This type of internal-combustion engine was invented by the German engineer Rudolf _____. The engine was designed to use coal dust as fuel, but now burns low-cost fuel oil. The engine is used in most trucks and a few automobiles.

11. Louis Pasteur was a nineteenth-century biologist and chemist who developed a process for killing microorganisms that caused disease or spoilage. This process involves heating a beverage or other food, such as milk, to a certain temperature for a specific length of time. What is the process called? _____

The Name Is the Same (cont.)

12. This popular item consists of meat or other food placed between two slices of bread. After many years, it was named after John Montagu, a gambler who liked to eat at the gambling table rather than to stop gambling. Montagu's title was the fourth Earl of _____.

13. Samuel _____ was an American inventor who patented a pistol with a revolving cylinder that was capable of firing six bullets, one after the other.

14. Robert Wilhelm _____ was a Prussian chemist and physicist who invented a gas burner that is used in many chemistry laboratories.

15. Scientists measure the seismic waves from an earthquake using a scale devised in 1935 by the American seismologist, Charles F. _____.

16. In 1858, John _____ patented a wide-mouthed glass jar with a screw neck that is used for canning and preserving food.

17. Dr. Henry _____, an American thoracic surgeon, developed a maneuver to help a person who is choking on a foreign object.

18. Adolphe Sax, a Belgian, put a clarinet mouthpiece on a brass instrument, added some keys, and produced an instrument that produced a mellow sound. This instrument is called a _____.

19. This swimming suit was invented in 1946 by two Frenchmen. They named the very small suit after an island where the atomic bomb was tested. Its name was _____.

20. Henry _____, a nineteenth-century British Army officer and inventor, devised an artillery shell containing metal balls that exploded above enemy troops. The metal fragments from a bomb still carry his name.

21. This invention is a kind of rigid airship, sometimes called a dirigible. It was named after Count Ferdinand von _____.

22. This lightweight, compact, submachine gun is manufactured by Israel Military Industries and was named after its designer, Usiel Gal. _____

23. This cast-iron heating stove, which was shaped like a fireplace, was invented by Benjamin _____, writer, inventor, and patriot.

24. This classic French dessert consists of three layers of flaky puff pastry that are filled with pastry cream and whipped cream and topped with a coating of sugar. It was named after the Emperor of France, _____ Bonaparte.

25. James _____, (1797–1868), was a British general who led the charge of the Light Brigade against the Russians in the Crimean War. A sweater that opens down the full length of the front is named after him.

9

Name: _____   Date: _____

Puzzle: Leonardo da Vinci

N E R O E D T O S H A

S   **W**

P   **M**

N   **L**

O   **S**

O   **I**

O   **I**

T   **P**

R   **H**

S   **U**

I U S R T P H A E S P

Leonardo da Vinci

    Leonardo da Vinci was an Italian who had many interests and abilities. He was a painter, sculptor, architect, engineer, and scientist. His new ideas in the area of painting influenced the course of Italian art for years after his death. Among some of his most famous paintings are *The Last Supper* and the *Mona Lisa*. He also excelled in astronomy, mathematics, engineering, botany, architecture, and geology. Da Vinci's inventions were years ahead of his time. His designs of some inventions technically could not have been completed in the period of time in which he lived; however, they were created centuries later by others. Some examples include the parachute, submarine, contact lenses, helicopter, and mechanical saw.

    Da Vinci once said something about education. Do you know what this quote was? It is hidden in the frame around the picture of da Vinci shown above. To discover the quote, you must go around the frame twice, reading every *other* letter. Where do you start, and which way do you read around the frame? That's what you have to figure out!

Answer: _____

Name: _____ Date: _____

Freshwater Fish

Fish are a group of animals that live in water. They are able to breathe underwater because they have gills. Most fish have fins for swimming and scales for protection.

Mudskipper

Pupfish

1. When a male mudskipper wants a mate, it:
   A. Selects one based on size.
   B. Kidnaps a female.
   C. Goes to a "dating school."
   D. Does push-ups.

2. If you keep a goldfish in a dark room, it will eventually:
   A. Die.   B. Grow smaller.
   C. Turn white.   D. Lose its ability to breathe.

3. The archer fish gets its meals of insects by:
   A. Using a disguise.   B. Spitting at them.
   C. Stealing.   D. Bartering.

4. The buriti palm of South America is often planted by:
   A. Birds.   B. Fish.
   C. Other palm trees.   D. Monkeys.

5. One species of the pupfish is unusual because:
   A. It can be a mother or a father.   B. It can fly.
   C. It grows up to become a dogfish.   D. It lives in the desert.

6. In order to find their way, the elephant-trunk fish of Africa and the Amazon knife-fish of South America:
   A. Use a flashlight.   B. Use a seeing-eye snail.
   C. Memorize locations.   D. Use radar, powered by electricity.

7. An African lungfish can survive out of water for:
   A. Four hours.   B. Four weeks.
   C. Four months.   D. Four years.

8. The walking catfish got its name because:
   A. It can walk on land.   B. It walks underwater.
   C. It can walk on water.   D. It looks as if it has legs.

9. A person can find out the age of a fish by:
   A. The size of its eyes.   B. Checking its size.
   C. Looking at its scales.   D. The length of its fins.

11

Name: _____ Date: _____

Freshwater Fish (cont.)

10. All Amazon molly fish are:
    A. Black.   B. Perfectly round.
    C. Female.   D. Born on land.

11. The lamprey eel builds a nest made of:
    A. Seaweed.   B. Stones.
    C. Mud.   D. Empty crab shells.

12. Male and female discus fish keep their young fish:
    A. In their mouths.   B. In shells.
    C. On leashes.   D. In cages of seaweed.

13. A pregnant goldfish is called a:
    A. Mollycoddle.   B. Twit.
    C. Dunce.   D. Big Mama.

14. There is a fish living in the Amazon River called "quatro ojos," which means *four eyes*. It
    was given this name because:
    A. Its two eyes are divided.   B. It looks as if it is wearing glasses.
    C. It has four large spots on its head. D. It has two large eyes on its head.

15. Piranhas live in large groups called:
    A. Schools.   B. Packs.
    C. Shoals.   D. Congresses.

Freshwater Fish—Answers

1. **D. Does push-ups.** The mudskipper is a fish that is about six inches long. It lives in swamps and on mud flats. It is able to walk, climb, and skip in and out of the water with its long, large fins. Both male and female mudskippers look similar except when it is time to breed. The male becomes very colorful and tries to attract a female by raising up on its pectoral fins in front of the female. It continues to move up and down until a female shows interest. Then the male leads the female into a burrow where the female lays her eggs, and the male fertilizes them.

2. **C. Turn white.** The goldfish breed was developed in China over 2,000 years ago. Europeans did not know of their existence until Marco Polo discovered them. If they are taken care of, goldfish can live for 40 years. Goldfish lose their color if they are kept in dim light or if they are placed in a body of running water, such as a stream. They remain gold only when they have adequate light and are kept in a pond or bowl.

3. **B. Spitting at them.** The archer fish is found in both freshwater and saltwater rivers in India, Asia, and northern Australia. It usually stays near the surface so it can find insects on vegetation above the surface of the water. When it sees an insect on a branch just above the water, it spits a jet of water out of its mouth, knocking the insect into the water, where the fish devours it. An archer fish can hit an insect five feet away.

4. **B. Fish.** The buriti is a palm that can grow up to 90 feet tall. It grows in the Amazon rain forest. The fruit is eaten by tapirs, jaguars, deer, parrots, and many other creatures of the rain forest. In the wild, this very popular tree relies on catfish to plant its seeds. When the forest floor is flooded by the heavy rain, the fruit of the buriti palm falls into the water that surrounds its trunk. The fruit is swallowed by catfish and eventually spreads to other shallow areas. When the water recedes, the seeds spring to life, and new buriti palm trees begin to grow.

5. **D. It lives in the desert.** Most people don't think of fish when they think of the desert, but in the Nevada desert, there is a small pool of water at the bottom of a cave that is home to the Devil's Hole pupfish. The pool is fed by a spring and is about the size of a swimming pool. There are about 500 pupfish in it. Over 12,000 years ago, this area wasn't a desert, but was a cool, wet area with lakes and rivers. Over time, the climate changed. It became hotter and drier, and the rivers and lakes evaporated. However, the pool that is home for the pupfish remained because the pool was fed by a spring. As a result, the fish survived. Pupfish eat algae from a submerged limestone shelf where they also spawn. The pupfish survived in this small, isolated environment for thousands of years, but in the 1970s, humans threatened its extinction. As agriculture began using the water table for irrigation, the area for the limestone shelf that sustained the pupfish decreased. The pupfish were saved by a court ruling regulating water pumping. The United States Supreme Court established a water level for Devil's Hole that would ensure the pupfish could survive in the future. Meanwhile, researchers have built similar habitats in the desert and have transferred a few pupfish to these habitats. This will help the species survive, in case there is a natural or manmade disaster at the original site.

6. **D. Use radar, powered by electricity.** The Amazon knife-fish and the African elephant-trunk fish use electricity to guide them and find prey. Nature has made it possible for them to generate an electric field around themselves, and they are able to determine what is near them by the pulses that bounce back.

Freshwater Fish—Answers (cont.)

7. **D. Four years.** Whenever a river or lake dries up, most of the fish die from a lack of oxygen. Their gills are designed to get oxygen from water, not air. When the water disappears, they suffocate. There are some fish, however, that in addition to gills, or sometimes in place of gills, have developed the ability to breathe atmospheric air. One such fish is called the lungfish. These fish look like eels and are found in Africa, Australia, and South America. Some reach lengths of over six feet. They often live in shallow lakes where there is little oxygen, so they must come to the surface to breathe. As the lake or swamp begins to dry up, the lungfish builds a burrow 24 inches deep and seals itself inside. It leaves a small air passage from the burrow to the top so it can get oxygen from above. African lungfish can survive for up to four years without water in these burrows, although rain often comes within a few months. During the spawning season, the South American and African lungfish build a nest for their young. After the female deposits the eggs, the male protects the nest until the eggs have hatched.

8. **A. It can walk on land.** The walking catfish cannot only walk on land, it can breathe air when it is out of water. These catfish live in ponds or pools that sometimes disappear when there is a drought. When this occurs, the catfish can leave the water that is disappearing and move to another place by using its pectoral fins as legs. If there is no other water available, the walking catfish will bury itself in mud and remain there until rains replenish its pond.

   The walking catfish is not native to the United States. It is a freshwater species originally from Southeast Asia. It was brought into the United States by tropical fish breeders. Some either escaped or were released in southern Florida in the 1960s. They are now thriving in the Everglades and are spreading to other areas where they prey on native fish.

9. **C. Looking at its scales.** Fish have growth rings similar to trees. Each year of the fish's life is represented by a pair of rings. Summer is represented by wider, lighter rings, while winter is represented by darker, narrow rings.

10. **C. Female.** There are no male Amazon mollies. The Amazon molly from Central America is related to the guppy. This race of female fish never gives birth to males. In order to reproduce, once a year the Amazon molly borrows a male of a closely related species—the sailfin molly—in order to have offspring. The Amazon molly has eggs with a complete set of chromosomes. The male does not actually fertilize the female's eggs, but activates cell division, so the offspring inherit nothing from the male. All of the offspring are identical to the mother. In other words, they are clones. Each offspring inherits the same traits, because there has not been a mixture of genes that could have been inherited from the father. Each generation continues to be a clone of all the generations that have gone before.

   Since the Amazon molly is related to the guppy, the mother must protect her brood from cannibalism. Male guppies are cannibalistic—they eat their own young. When a female starts to give birth to her live babies, the male will swim under the female and eat them as they are born. The Amazon molly prevents cannibalism by maintaining her own territory. She leaves her territory only to mate with the sailfin molly and then returns to her territory. If the male tries to follow her, she beats him with her fins and rams him until he leaves.

14

Freshwater Fish—Answers (cont.)

11. **B. Stones.** The lamprey eel spends part of its time in the ocean and part of its time in fresh water. Each March, the lamprey leaves the ocean and goes to where the rivers empty into the ocean. Here it waits for a fish called a shad. It attaches to the shad and will stay attached as the shad swims upstream to spawn. During the journey, the lamprey will suck the eggs of the shad. By June, the female lamprey will leave the shad and start building a nest of rocks in a swift current, first hollowing out an area, carrying stones with her mouth until the nest measures four feet around and three feet high. She moves these large, heavy stones by sticking her mouth to the stone and pulling it into place. The male lamprey stays close by, but does not help. When the female is finished building the nest, the lamprey lays her eggs in it, swims away, and dies. Whenever they hatch, the young lampreys go ashore and bury themselves in the sand. There are two other interesting facts about the lamprey. If put out in the sun, the lamprey melts like butter, and only a grease spot remains. Also, the lamprey eel is actually not an eel at all, but an eel-shaped fish.

12. **C. On leashes.** Discus fish are flat, freshwater fishes. They are very good parents. They nurse their babies. They have cells in their skin that secrete a mucus to nourish the babies. While a baby is learning to swim, it has threads that are attached from it to one of its parents. After a while, the parent that is leading the young discus fish on the thread will swim to its mate and shake off the thread, and the baby becomes attached to the other parent to continue the swimming lesson.

13. **B. Twit.**

14. **A. Its two eyes are divided.** While this fish has only two eyes, the eyes are able to operate as if there were four. Each eye is divided, so there is an upper and a lower part. When the fish swims just below the surface of the water, it is able to check for food underneath the water, and at the same time, it watches for predators above the water.

15. **C. Shoals.** Found in the Amazon River, piranhas are **carnivorous**, which means they eat the flesh of animals. Piranhas are noted for their strong jaws with sharp, triangular teeth they use to tear their prey apart before eating it. They hunt in groups of more than 100, called shoals. Most of the time, the shoal swims into a school of fish. While many of their prey swim away, some are isolated and attacked. The small prey are swallowed whole, while large prey fish have big chunks torn from them. While it is rare, piranhas sometimes attack large animals that come to the water to drink. There have been reports of piranhas attacking humans, but these instances are very rare.

15

Name: _____ Date: _____

Ocean Creatures: General

Ocean covers almost three-fourths of the surface of the earth. The oceans of the world are connected and composed of salt water. The oceans are home to most of the animal and plant life on Earth.

1. Whenever a sea cucumber encounters an enemy, it:
    A. Changes colors.   B. Pretends to be a sea snake.
    C. Pretends to be a sea zucchini.   D. Spits out its intestines.

2. Which of the following does a jellyfish have?
    A. Heart.   B. Bones.
    C. Brain.   D. Nerves.

3. If a starfish is cut in two,:
    A. Each part will become a new starfish.   B. It will kill any fish that eats it.
    C. It will attract any shark within ten miles. D. Each piece will heal and live.

4. If you are stung by a jellyfish, which of the following should you *not* apply to the wound?
    A. Vinegar.   B. Rubbing alcohol.
    C. Meat tenderizer.   D. Water.

5. The starfish is the only animal capable of:
    A. Growing new body parts.   B. Turning its stomach inside-out.
    C. Changing its sex.   D. Changing its species.

6. Diving for sponges was once:
    A. An Olympic event.   B. Done by teenage girls.
    C. Taught to dolphins.   D. Only done by women.

7. Jellyfish can be kept in aquariums, but they must be kept in aquariums that are:
    A. Square.   B. Rectangular.
    C. Circular.   D. H-shaped.

8. Where are the eyes or eye spots located on a starfish?
    A. On the top of its head   B. On its stomach
    C. At the tip of each of its arms   D. On its antenna

9. Jellyfish are more than 95 percent:
    A. Water.   B. Gelatin.
    C. Plasma.   D. Fat.

Name: _____ Date: _____

Ocean Creatures: General (cont.)

10. One of the first drugs for treating cancer, cytosine arabinoside, was isolated from a:
    A. Starfish.   B. Hydra.
    C. Sponge.   D. Sea cucumber.

11. Hydras live underwater and move by:
    A. Walking on the ocean floor.   B. Turning cartwheels.
    C. Attaching to a fish.   D. Floating with the current.

12. The red-beard sponge contains a poison that is capable of:
    A. Killing a shark.   B. Stunning a whale.
    C. Killing viruses.   D. Curing paralysis.

13. How many eggs at a time do starfish release?
    A. 25,000   B. 250,000
    C. 2.5 million   D. 25 million

14. The black sea nettle provides the Pacific butterfish with food and protection. The silvery butterfish feeds on the plankton gathered by the jellyfish. When danger approaches, it:
    A. Sacrifices its life for the nettle.   B. Hides in the nettle's belly.
    C. Imitates a mackerel.   D. Changes color.

15. All European and American freshwater eels are born in:
    A. Stagnant pools.   B. The Sargasso Sea.
    C. Freshwater streams.   D. Whitewater rivers.

Ocean Creatures: General—Answers

1. **D. Spits out its intestines.** The sea cucumber is an animal, not a vegetable. It is about four inches long, dark in color, and sometimes has small bumps, just like a cucumber. Most species have several rows of tube feet covering their bodies, making them appear as if they are covered with worms. But while the appearance of the sea cucumber is unusual, it is not as unusual as its behavior. Whenever a cucumber is approached by a predator, it vomits its intestines through its mouth and anus. Some species also eject sticky filaments. This mixture of entrails and goo confuses the predator, and when the predator gets tangled up in the mess, the sea cucumber is able to escape. Strangely enough, the sea cucumber does not die, even though it does not have its intestines. It will begin to grow new ones and will eventually become as good as new. Chinese people enjoy eating soup made from the sea cucumber.

2. **D. Nerves.** Jellyfish have been on the earth for over 650 million years. They were here before dinosaurs. Jellyfish, or jellies as they are sometimes called, are very unusual creatures. They are beautiful, disk-shaped animals that are more than 95% water and have no bones, eyes, heart, or brain. They do have a network of nerve cells that helps them use jet propulsion to move, avoid danger, and find food. Most jellyfish do not live very long. Some live only a few weeks, while others may survive for a few years. Jellies are considered a delicacy by many.

3. **A. Each part will become a new starfish.** Most species of starfish, also known as sea stars, reproduce **heterosexually.** This means that both males and females are needed to produce young. Some species take care of their eggs and young, while others release their eggs into the water. Some species reproduce by **hermaphroditism,** which means that one creature is both male and female and can reproduce without a mate. A few reproduce **asexually** by dividing the body; this is called **fission.** Regardless of the specific method of reproduction, if a starfish loses an arm or two, it can grow new ones. This is called **regeneration.**

4. **D. Water.** If you are stung by a jellyfish, it is best to apply vinegar or alcohol immediately to keep the poison from activating. Next, put a paste of water and meat tenderizer on the wound. The meat tenderizer will break down the protein of the toxin and relieve the pain. Rinsing the wound with water could release more poison.

5. **B. Turning its stomach inside-out.** The starfish is the only animal that is able to turn its stomach inside-out. Starfish usually prey on mollusks. When a starfish advances toward its prey, it reverses its stomach, pushes it out through its mouth, and puts it under the shell of its prey. Then it consumes its victim by absorption.

6. **A. An Olympic event.** The sponge has long been a source of fascination for humans. Is it a plant or an animal? Early scientists thought it was probably a plant because of its appearance. It wasn't until the eighteenth century that scientists began to notice the animal features of sponges. Whether the sponge was an animal or a plant did not matter to countless civilizations. However, it was able to perform functions unlike any other thing in nature. Phoenicians and Egyptians harvested sponges and used them for many purposes. Ancient Greeks used sponges for padding their armor and helmets. Those

Ocean Creatures: General—Answers (cont.)

who dove for deep-water sponges were so strong and athletic that sponge-diving was introduced into the original Olympic Games.

7. **C. Circular.** Jellyfish are fragile animals and could easily get stuck in the corners of aquariums and tear themselves as they try to get loose. Therefore, most tanks that house jellyfish are circular.

8. **C. At the tip of each of its arms.**

9. **A. Water.**

10. **C. Sponge.**

11. **B. Turning cartwheels.**

12. **C. Killing viruses.** The natural sponge is an unusual animal with many beneficial properties. Since it does not burn, glassmakers use the sponge to wipe hot glass. Recent studies have discovered some medical benefits of the sponge as well. For example, the red-beard sponge contains a poison that kills many microbes and viruses, including the strong and aggressive staphylococcus that is resistant to penicillin. There is evidence that this sponge may be beneficial in the treatment of tuberculosis, bladder disease, and trench mouth.

13. **C. 2.5 million.**

14. **B. Hides in the nettle's belly.**

15. **B. The Sargasso Sea.** The Sargasso Sea is located in the central North Atlantic Ocean between the West Indies and the Azores. It is an unusual sea because it is surrounded not by land, but by the Atlantic Ocean. Its warm waters are very clear and blue and filled with seaweed. When Columbus first encountered the Sargasso Sea, he thought he was very close to shore because of the quantities of floating algae. Columbus's sailors were afraid their ships would get stuck in the seaweed. While the seaweed is not thick enough to stall a ship, the calm water of the Sargasso Sea fooled many early sailors into thinking it might. The Sargasso Sea is sometimes called a floating desert. While there are many small marine animals that live on and around the seaweed, there are few nutrients at the lower depths and, consequently, little life. For some reason, the Sargassso Sea is the spot in which eels from North America, Europe, and the Mediterranean come to mate, spawn, and then die. After they are born, the larvae will make the return journey to their respective countries, a journey that can last three years. Once they arrive, the males stay at the mouth of the river, and the females swim upstream to the lakes and ponds that are often found on islands. They stay there for ten to fifteen years and then swim back to the sea. The males and females then swim together back to the Sargasso Sea where the process is repeated.

Name: _____ Date: _____

 # Ocean Creatures: Saltwater Fish

Fish are cold-blooded vertebrate animals that live in either fresh or salt waters. Salt water covers 71 percent of the surface of the earth. In these oceans, a wide variety of fish have evolved in response to the environment in which they live.

1. The sea dragon of southern and eastern Australia, a relative of the sea horse, avoids predators by:
   A. Looking like seaweed.   B. Swimming fast.
   C. Looking like a dragon.   D. Disappearing.

2. The saber-toothed blenny fish gets some of its meals by:
   A. Pretending to be dead.   B. Stealing from other fish.
   C. Pretending to be a maid.   D. Growing it.

3. The clownfish is unusual in that it is able to:
   A. Amuse other fish.   B. Change its sex.
   C. Look like a clown.   D. Fly.

4. The sailfish is the ocean's fastest fish. It is capable of reaching speeds of:
   A. 28 miles per hour.   B. 48 miles per hour.
   C. 68 miles per hour.   D. 88 miles per hour.

5. A flying fish gets its name because it:
   A. Can fly like a bird.   B. Appears to fly.
   C. Looks like a fly.   D. Has wings.

6. The parrotfish sleeps in a:
   A. Tree.   B. Sleeping bag of slime.
   C. Whale's mouth.   D. Mud hut.

7. The hagfish is unusual because it attacks its prey:
   A. Only on Sunday.   B. Once a year.
   C. From the inside.   D. By hypnotism.

8. One unique feature of a flatfish is that its eyes:
   A. Are on the same side of its head.   B. Flash on or off, depending on the light.
   C. Are located on its tail.   D. Are inside its mouth.

9. The pufferfish contains a nerve poison that is 10,000 times more deadly than cyanide and is used in Japan as:
   A. Food.   B. A weapon of war.
   C. Rat poison.   D. Medicine.

20

Name: _____ Date: _____

Ocean Creatures: Saltwater Fish (cont.)

10. To the female, the male bearded anglerfish is a:
   A. Bully.
   B. Protector.
   C. Parasite.
   D. Teacher.

11. The anglerfish got its name because:
   A. Daniel Angler discovered it.
   B. It is shaped like an acute angle.
   C. It snares fish with a mucus net.
   D. It has a fishing rod on its head.

12. The polar fish's blood does not freeze in the cold waters of the Antarctic because:
   A. It is warm-blooded.
   B. Its blood has antifreeze in it.
   C. It never stops moving.
   D. It doesn't have any blood.

13. There is a "flashlight fish" that gets its name because:
   A. It is shaped like a flashlight.
   B. It glows in the dark.
   C. It has a built-in flashlight.
   D. It changes colors.

14. If a part of the starfish known as *Linckia laevigata* is cut off, the small piece will:
   A. Grow a new starfish.
   B. Be harvested by fishermen.
   C. Be used as a home by a crab.
   D. Kill any creature that eats it.

15. What is the world's largest living fish?
   A. Blue whale
   B. Mauve whale
   C. Sailfish
   D. Whale shark

16. The male gafftopsail catfish starves itself for up to eight weeks in order to:
   A. Become attractive to females.
   B. Preserve food for its mate.
   C. Look like a female gafftopsail.
   D. Hatch fish eggs.

17. The male sea horse is the one that:
   A. Gets pregnant.
   B. Lays the eggs.
   C. Builds the nests.
   D. Teaches the young to swim.

18. A male pipefish has:
   A. A flashlight on its nose.
   B. Whiskers shaped like a pipe.
   C. Two sets of eyes.
   D. A zipper in its abdomen.

19. The gurnard is a fish that:
   A. Can become invisible.
   B. Swims upside-down.
   C. Can kill a whale.
   D. Can predict a thunderstorm.

20. When black sea bass grow to be 9–13 inches long, 38 percent:
   A. Die.
   B. Become males.
   C. Spawn.
   D. Migrate to Ireland.

Name: _____ Date: _____

Ocean Creatures: Saltwater Fish (cont.)

21. The glass catfish:
    A. Is almost totally transparent.   B. Can shatter like glass.
    C. Is neither glass nor a catfish.   D. Was used as a glass by Native Americans.

22. Bombay duck is a food made from:
    A. Pickled duck.   B. Octopus.
    C. Dried fish.   D. Asian goose.

23. Which of the following did American Indians *not* burn for fuel?
    A. Wood   B. Buffalo chips
    C. Fish   D. Fire ants

24. The lemon shark grows approximately _____ new teeth per year.
    A. 24   B. 240
    C. 2,400   D. 24,000

25. Sharkskin has sometimes been used as:
    A. A covering for canoes.   B. Material for swimming suits.
    C. Sandpaper.   D. To make shark repellent.

26. Many species of sharks are being hunted to extinction because fisherman are harvesting the sharks':
    A. Meat.   B. Skin.
    C. Teeth.   D. Fins.

Ocean Creatures: Saltwater Fish—Answers (cont.)

1. **A. Looking like seaweed.** Sea dragons grow 18 inches long and are covered with skin flaps that look like seaweed. These skin flaps are loose and sway with the current, making the disguise appear real. Sea dragons live in kelp beds where they are almost undetectable. In the event a sea dragon is seen by a predator, it is protected by bony armor and long dorsal spines, which make it almost impossible to eat. The sea dragon is unusual in another way; the male broods the eggs. The fertilized eggs are fastened to its tail and stay there until they hatch.

2. **C. Pretending to be a maid.** Another fish called the *wrasse*, which is sometimes called the cleaner fish, performs a valuable service to bigger fish. The larger fish opens its mouth and lets the wrasse swim in. Once inside, the wrasse eats dead skin, parasites, lice, and other irritants. It also cleans the external parts of the larger fish. When it is finished, the wrasse swims away. The larger fish, in order to stay healthy, relies on the cleaning activities of the wrasse. In fact, each day, hundreds of fish, both large and small, hunt for the wrasse to clean them. While the larger fish are being cleaned, they remain still.

    There is another fish that also hangs around these cleaning areas. The saber-toothed blenny looks and swims like a wrasse. It uses these similarities to get close to these fish. Since the larger fish have had a good experience with the wrasse, they welcome the approach of the sabre-toothed blenny. This is a mistake, because once it is close, the blenny takes a bite out of the larger fish.

3. **B. Change its sex.** Clownfish have become a very popular aquarium fish since the release of the Disney movie, *Finding Nemo.* In the wild, clownfish live on Australia's Great Barrier Reef. Only the dominant pair of the school are sexually active and reproduce. If the dominant female dies, her mate, the dominant breeding male, changes sex and becomes a female. Then the largest non-breeder male takes the male's place as the dominant breeding male.

4. **C. 68 miles per hour.** That is faster than the speed limit on most U.S. highways. The sailfish is a game fish found in warm and temperate waters in many oceans. The sailfish has a large dorsal fin that is blue and is silver below. Extending from its snout is a long spear. Sailfish hunt in groups. They frighten their prey by raising their dorsal fins. When they are in pursuit of tuna, mackerel, or other creatures upon which they feed, they put their pectoral fins to their sides and put their large dorsal fins against their backs. When they streamline themselves in this way, they are the fastest fish in the world.

5. **B. It appears to fly.** The flying fish, which is found in tropical and subtropical seas, does not fly in the same way in which a bird flies. It actually glides. This is a technique the fish has developed in order to escape its enemies. When it is being pursued, it will swim very fast and then go to the surface. When it reaches a speed of about 20 miles an hour, it will put its fins against its body and then launch itself into the air. While in the air, it opens its large pectoral fins that act as wings, and it glides. It will glide for hundreds of feet just above the surface of the water. As it loses speed, it sinks back to the surface of the water where it moves its tail from side to side, giving it more power to take off again. It may repeat this gliding action several times.

6. **B. Sleeping bag of slime.** Found in tropical and subtropical oceans, the parrotfish has bright colors and fused front teeth that look like a bird's beak. The parrotfish protects

Ocean Creatures: Saltwater Fish—Answers (cont.)

itself by staying inside a sleeping bed of slime. It creates this cocoon by secreting a slimy mucus that covers its body. The sleeping bag not only protects the parrotfish, it also keeps the fish's odor inside, so predators cannot find it.

7. **C. From the inside.** The hagfish is an unusual sea creature. It is shaped like an eel and does not have jaws or a stomach. Its eyes are concealed beneath its skin. It is about 32 inches long. The hagfish is sometimes called a slime eel because it secretes a lot of slime when it is handled. What makes it unusual, however, is the way in which it attacks its prey. The hagfish diet consists of fish that are either dying or are already dead. The hagfish scrapes a hole in the side of the fish, using its sharp teeth. It then enters the body and begins feeding. Once inside the body, it consumes its victim from the inside out. In order to discourage other scavengers from feeding on its prey, the hagfish will create a cocoon of slime around the body of the fish. The slime is so thick, it blocks the gills of other fish who might try to compete with hagfish for the prey. Hagfish are disliked by commercial fisherman because the hagfish sometimes attack fish caught on a line or net and consume it before the fishermen are able to bring in their catch.

8. **A. Are on the same side of its head.** Flatfish are a type of flattened fish, some of which live in fresh water, and some of which live in the ocean. Some common flatfish are turbot, flounder, sole, and halibut. Their flat bodies help them avoid predators by hiding on the ocean floor. Another feature that helps some flatfish avoid predators is their ability to change colors in order to blend into their background. When a flatfish is being pursued, it will agitate the water, causing a curtain of sand that will make it hard to see. Then it will dive to the bottom of the ocean where its flat body will change to the color of the sand. As the sand drifts back to the bottom, some falls on the flatfish, partially covering it up. It is almost undetectable. With both of its eyes on the same side of its head, it is able to stay on the bottom and see when it is safe to leave.

9. **A. Food.** Mostly found in subtropical and tropical waters, pufferfish are also known as blowfish, swellfish, and globefish. They have been named pufferfish because, when threatened, they expand to twice their normal size by taking in water. Many parts of the blowfish, including its skin, reproductive organs, and digestive system, contain an extremely strong, deadly, paralyzing poison that protects it from predators. There is no known antidote for this poison. In Japan, where the fish is called fugu, it is considered a delicacy. Only specially trained chefs prepare this fish. In spite of their caution, many Japanese have died from eating this poisonous fish.

10. **C. Parasite.** It is important for the survival of the bearded anglerfish to find a mate. If successful, the female will provide her mate with food for his entire life. While there are over 200 species of anglerfish, the male bearded anglerfish is only one-fourth the size of the female. Once the male finds a female, he bites into her body, and eventually his mouth will fuse to her skin; their blood supplies then become connected. Once connected, the male begins to deteriorate. His eyes become smaller and eventually disappear, as do his internal organs. From then on, the male is a parasite, relying on the female for nourishment.

11. **D. It has a fishing rod on its head.** *Angler* is another name for a fisherman. The anglerfish was named because it fishes for its meals in a manner similar to humans. It uses a "fishing rod," which is actually the foremost spine of its dorsal fin and is located on

Ocean Creatures: Saltwater Fish—Answers (cont.)

top of its head. On the tip of its spine, or fishing rod, is a fleshy area that the anglerfish uses as "bait," or a "lure." Fish are attracted to this "bait," and when they come close enough to investigate, the anglerfish swallows them. Only female anglerfish have a "fishing rod." Some are short, and some are long. The "bait" is bright and often glows.

12. **B. Its blood has antifreeze in it.** In the Antarctic's icy, salty, sea water, most fish would freeze solid. The polar fish avoids this fate because its blood contains a special protein that acts as an antifreeze and maintains the fish's blood at 27.5°. This temperature is adequate to enable the polar fish to survive.

13. **C. It has a built-in flashlight.** Although the flashlight fish appears to wear a flashlight, which it uses to send out light to explore the ocean at night, the light is not really part of the fish itself. The light comes from glowing bacteria living under the eyes and on the skin of the fish. The flashlight fish lives in caves and only leaves at night. With this light, it has an advantage over the other creatures on the ocean floor. Its "flashlight" enables it to attract other fish in order for it to eat. The fish is able to turn the light off by drawing a fold of black skin over its eyes.

In 1967, just after the Arab-Israeli conflict, there was a school of flashlight fish swimming in the Gulf of Eilat. The fish had their lights blinking on and off. Israeli troops, who were patrolling the coastline, saw the light and thought there were enemy frogmen in the area. They threw grenades at the lights, and dead flashlight fish washed ashore.

14. **A. Grow a new starfish.** This species of starfish can grow back a completely new body from a single piece that is less than one-half-inch long. This species is sometimes called the blue linckia sea star, blue sea star, blue starfish, or the comet sea star. It has a bright-blue body and is found on and around reefs. While the *Linckia laevigata* can regrow a new starfish from a small part that is separated from its body, it only performs this miracle in the wild. Some people keep this species in aquariums. The regrowth of new bodies is very rare when kept in captivity.

15. **D. Whale shark.** This huge but harmless shark can weigh up to 20 tons and grow to 50 feet in length. The blue whale, the largest animal now living and possibly the largest that has ever lived, is not a fish. It is a mammal. The blue whale can weigh 150 tons and grow to 100 feet in length The heart of a blue whale weighs about 1,500 pounds—about the size of a Volkswagen Beetle.

16. **D. Hatch fish eggs.** The male gafftopsail catfish does not eat because it carries about 50 eggs in its mouth, protecting them until they hatch. Other species do the same. This practice is called mouthbrooding.

17. **A. Gets pregnant.** There are about 35 species of sea horses whose scientific genus name is *Hippocampus*. *Hippocampus* is a Greek word that means "bent horse." Sea horses live in temperate and tropical waters and range in size from two to fourteen inches. What sets them apart from other fish—in addition to their unusual appearance—is that the male is the one who gets pregnant. A female sea horse deposits her eggs into a

Ocean Creatures: Saltwater Fish—Answers (cont.)

pouch underneath the male's tail. The male fertilizes the eggs. The eggs develop into embryos and remain in the pouch until they are born. Sea horses can have hundreds of babies at one time.

18. **D. A zipper in its abdomen.** In the abdomen, or on the lower side of the tail of the male pipefish, is a slit that is the opening to a pouch. Into this pouch, the female deposits her fertilized eggs. The opening is then zipped closed for sixteen days until the young hatch. The folds of the pouch then zip back open, and the young are able to leave.

19. **D. Can predict a thunderstorm.** The gurnard grunts very loudly whenever a thunderstorm is about to occur. Many fishermen believe so strongly in the gurnard's ability to predict a storm that whenever they hear the fish grunting, they head their boats for home.

20. **B. Become males.** Black sea bass are female when they are young, but after spawning, about 38 percent in the mid-Atlantic change their sex and become males. When they spawn, black sea bass produce about 280,000 eggs that float together in a globe shape.

21. **A. Is almost totally transparent.** The muscles of the glass catfish are transparent, but their bones are not, so one can see the thin bones of their skeletons. Their major organs and intestines are bunched together in the front end of the fish. These are not transparent either.

22. **C. Dried fish.** Bombay duck is a small Asiatic fish that is used as a relish in India. It is also called bummalo. Bummalo is a slimy fish that is caught in November and December and then processed until March.

23. **D. Fire ants.** The candlefish of the Pacific is used literally as a candle by the Native Americans of North America. They thread a wick through the fish's body, and when the wick is lit, the body fat burns steadily, or the whole fish can be set on fire to be used as a torch.

24. **D. 24,000.** There are over 300 species of sharks who shed and replace teeth at different rates. A shark's teeth are never worn down because they don't last long enough. A shark sheds its teeth and grows new ones. Sharks' teeth are so sharp that natives of the South Pacific have been known to shave with them. The great white shark has teeth that are as hard as steel.

25. **C. Sandpaper.** Shark scales look like small shark teeth and, in fact, they are. Scientists believe the teeth of sharks evolved from changes in the sharks' scales. Sharkskin is also very tough and pliable. When properly prepared, sharkskin is made into fine leather goods, such as purses, shoes, boots, and wallets.

26. **D. Fins.** While some fisherman hunt sharks for their skin and meat, hunting them for their fins can make a fisherman more money and, consequently, has greatly decreased the number of sharks available. The fins are used to make shark-fin soup, which is very popular in China. A bowl of high-quality shark-fin soup can cost more than $100. Fishermen who specialize in hunting sharks for their fins will catch the sharks, cut off the fins, and drop them back into the ocean to die.

Name: _____ Date: _____

Fish Idioms

Directions: An **idiom** is a figure of speech or an expression that is sometimes used to express an idea. Here is a group of expressions that uses
the word "fish" or refers to a fish or other creature that lives in water. Under
each idiom, explain in your own words what the expression means.

1. Swims like a fish

    _____

2. A pretty kettle of fish

    _____

3. Packed in like sardines

    _____

4. Drink like a fish

    _____

5. A red herring

    _____

6. Fishing for a compliment

    _____

7. A loan shark

    _____

8. Bigger fish to fry

    _____

9. Like a fish out of water

    _____

10. Not the only fish in the sea

    _____

11. Fishing in troubled waters

    _____

12. A whale of a time

    _____

13. As slippery as an eel

    _____

14. As happy as a clam

    _____

Name: _____ Date: _____

Ocean Creatures: Mollusks

Mollusks are a group of soft-bodied animals that includes snails, clams, squids, octopuses, and sea slugs. Many mollusks have shells. Snails are called **univalves** because they have only one shell. Two-shelled mollusks are called **bivalves**. Some examples of bivalves are oysters, clams, and scallops. In addition to being used for food, bivalves also produce pearls. Not all mollusks have shells. Some may have had shells in previous generations but have lost them as they have evolved. Squids and octopuses fall into this category.

1. There are some desert snails that can sleep for:
   A. One to two months.
   B. Six to twelve months.
   C. One to two years.
   D. Two to three years.

2. Octopuses have three _____ and _____ blood.
   A. Hearts, blue
   B. Eyes, no
   C. Mates, green
   D. Antennae, no

3. Snails can have _____ teeth.
   A. 5
   B. 500
   C. 5,000
   D. 50,000

4. Oysters and mussels are used in many countries:
   A. To monitor ocean pollution.
   B. For money.
   C. As building materials.
   D. As pets.

5. Liguus tree snails are called:
   A. Slugs.
   B. Morning buds.
   C. Living jewels.
   D. Summer pearls.

6. How long does it take a deep-sea clam to grow 0.3 inches?
   A. 1 day
   B. 1 year
   C. 10 years
   D. 100 years

7. In France, as well as in other countries, there are farms that raise snails for:
   A. Pest control.
   B. Snail races.
   C. Food.
   D. Jewelry.

8. The Dumbo octopus got its name because:
   A. It looks like Dumbo the elephant.
   B. *Dumbo* means "large" in Italian.
   C. It is not very smart.
   D. Giovanni Dumbolini discovered it.

9. For which of the following have the shells of windowpane oysters shells *not* been used?
   A. Windowpanes.
   B. Wind chimes.
   C. Lampshades.
   D. Musical instruments.

Name: _____ Date: _____

Ocean Creatures: Mollusks (cont.)

10. Octopuses are the world's _____ invertebrates (animals without backbones).
    A. Largest   B. Smartest   C. Tastiest   D. Deadliest

11. Many red octopuses live in:
    A. Seaweed.   B. Beer bottles.   C. Clamshells.   D. Dead whales.

12. Snail shells may be:
    A. Made of calcium, stone, or plastic.   B. Used to prevent Alzheimer's disease.
    C. Used to catch whales.   D. Left-handed or right-handed.

13. When an octopus gets angry, it:
    A. Attacks.   B. Turns blue.
    C. Makes a smoke screen.   D. "Plays dead."

14. For which one of the following are cuttlefish bones *not* used?
    A. Bird food supplement   B. Tooth polish
    C. Sharpening instruments   D. Women's hats

15. Cephalopods, a group that includes octopuses and cuttlefish, communicate by:
    A. Pantomime.   B. Changing colors.   C. Touching.   D. Sounds.

16. Scallops swim by:
    A. Back-drafting.   B. Jet propulsion.   C. Whirling.   D. Slithering.

17. The snail is:
    A. All male.   B. All female.
    C. Both male and female.   D. Neither male nor female.

18. What is a winkle?
    A. An edible sea snail   B. A snail shell
    C. A baby starfish   D. A string of octopus eggs

19. When they are exposed to stressful situations, some octopuses:
    A. Explode.   B. Eat their arms off.
    C. Have a stroke.   D. Make a screeching sound.

20. After an oyster produces its young, it often:
    A. Dies.   B. Changes from male to female.
    C. Kills them.   D. Abandons them.

21. The European oyster, which lives just off the coast of Denmark, changes its _____ about every five years.
    A. Mate   B. Shell   C. Location   D. Sex

Name: _____ Date: _____

Ocean Creatures: Mollusks (cont.)

22. A marine snail called the tethys is about one foot long. When it lays eggs, it lays about 40,000 eggs in:
    A. One minute.   B. Ten minutes.   C. Thirty minutes.   D. One hour.

23. Some land snails court each other by:
    A. Changing colors.
    B. Throwing rocks at each other.
    C. Shooting darts at each other.
    D. Waving their antennae at each other.

24. The mimic octopus got its name because:
    A. It looks like a rock.
    B. It impersonates other sea creatures.
    C. Because of the sound it makes.
    D. It is found in the Mimicia Sea.

25. In order to breathe, the apple snail:
    A. Comes up for air every 15 minutes.
    B. Has gills.
    C. Snorkels.
    D. Builds a cave with air bubbles.

26. After a female octopus lays her eggs, she:
    A. Immediately mates again.
    B. Starves herself to death.
    C. Gives them to the male to watch.
    D. Abandons the eggs.

27. A squid is capable of:
    A. Preying on sharks.
    B. Changing its sex.
    C. Becoming transparent.
    D. Mating with an octopus.

28. In order to escape a shark that swims fast, some squids may:
    A. Fly.
    B. Walk on water.
    C. Throw small fish at the shark.
    D. Make sounds like a dolphin.

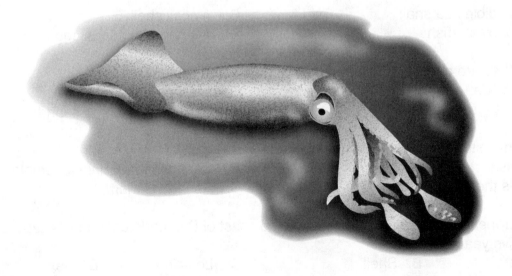

Ocean Creatures: Mollusks—Answers

1. **D. Two to three years.** Snails go to sleep while the weather is very cold. This is called **hibernation.** When they hibernate, snails bury themselves and then close up the entrance to their shells with slime that becomes hard. This tough covering will protect the snail from predators. A small hole permits air to come in.

2. **A. Hearts, blue.** Octopuses tire quickly because their blood does not carry oxygen well. In order to make up for this, the octopus has three hearts to pump its blood around.

3. **D. 50,000.** In a snail's mouth is something called a **radula,** which is used to grind food. The radula could be described as a rough tongue. It is like a file with row after row of teeth that are used to scrape the flowers and leaves the snail eats. The radula continues to grow, and new rows of teeth are always being formed.

4. **A. To monitor ocean pollution.** Since oysters and mussels do not move and they feed by filtering particles from the water, they accumulate chemicals and other pollutants. By examining these creatures, scientists are able to find out a lot about what is in the water.

5. **C. Living jewels.** Florida tree snails live on the bark of hardwood trees. Once they were plentiful, but today they are rare. Tree snails are two to three inches long and have brightly colored spiraled shells. These beautiful shells have been a popular collector's item. Overcollection is one of the reasons the population of this species has been greatly reduced. Another reason is the increased usage of insect spraying, as humans begin to build in the areas where the tree snail used to thrive. Furthermore, Hurricane Andrew in 1992 damaged the protected snail habitat in Big Cypress National Preserve and Everglades National Park. In the areas hit hardest by the hurricane, as many as 80% of the trees in which the tree snails lived were destroyed. These factors have caused the Florida Game and Freshwater Fish Commission to name the Florida tree snail a *Species of Special Concern.* This designation protects them, dead or alive, from collectors.

6. **D. 100 years.** The small *Tindaria callistiformis* may be among the slowest-growing, yet longest-living species, but there is another bivalve that lives even longer. The longest-living bivalve is the ocean quahog, *Arctica islandica.* It may also be the longest-lived animal. Samples dredged from the Atlantic reveal that many live for over 150 years. One bivalve found had lived 220 years.

7. **C. Food.** Snails have long been eaten. Archaeological excavations have revealed that prehistoric humans feasted on snails. In ancient Rome, there were snail farms where snails were carefully grown for feasts. Snails were even used as folk medicine. Today, snails are eaten in many countries. In some countries, snails are referred to as **escargot,** which is pronounced *es-car-go.* If you order escargot in a restaurant, you will be served a land snail, which is usually served in the shell, with a sauce of melted butter and garlic. It is very expensive.

8. **A. It looks like Dumbo the elephant.** The Dumbo octopus lives in deep water and is the size of a basketball. It looks very much like the Walt Disney cartoon elephant, with a big head and fins instead of ears.

9. **D. Musical instruments.** The kapis is a bivalve mollusk with a **translucent,** not **transparent,** shell and small body. The kapis is prized for its shell, which can be made into

Ocean Creatures: Mollusks—Answers (cont.)

windowpanes. These panes are ideal for filtering out the hot tropical sun and are strong enough to withstand hurricanes. The shells are also used for lampshades, chandeliers, flower vases, and many other items. The meat of the mollusk is eaten because it is an excellent source of protein.

10. **B. Smartest.** Octopuses have the most developed brain of the invertebrates and have long-term and short-term memories similar to vertebrates. Controlled experiments have shown that not only are they able to solve problems, but they are also able to remember how they solved them and repeat what they have learned.

11. **B. Beer bottles.** Since the octopus has no shell or backbone, it is able to fit into very small and tight spots. The natural habitat of octopuses is a lair or den under a rock, ledge, or other small opening. Today, however, there is a lot of trash in the sea. Beer bottles, soda bottles, cans, tires, and many other types of rubbish provide hiding places and homes for sea animals. Many red octopuses live in beer or soda bottles. The bottle's small opening and strong walls give it better protection than it would have by hiding under a rock. While the small red octopus likes to live in beer bottles, the Atlantic green octopus prefers children's shoes.

12. **D. Left-handed or right-handed.** Snail shells may be left-handed, which means they spiral in a counterclockwise direction, or they may be right-handed, which means they spiral in a clockwise direction. Most snail species are right-handed.

13. **C. Makes a smoke screen.** When frightened or threatened, the octopus reacts like other cephalopods. It squirts ink at its enemy. This produces a black cloud, making the octopus difficult to see and enabling it to escape.

14. **D. Women's hats.** Cuttlefish bones or cuttlebones are the internal shells that protect the internal organs of the cuttlefish. Cuttlefish bones are porous, white, chalky, and rich in calcium. The cuttlefish bones are placed in the cages of birds as a valuable source of calcium. When ground into a fine powder, cuttlebone is used to clean teeth and polish silver. It is also used to sharpen fine instruments, and silversmiths use it to make molds for casting. The ink of the cuttlefish, which is called sepia, was once used for writing and drawing. Sepia is not black, but a dark brown.

15. **B. Changing colors.** Cephalopods are able to control the color of their skin when their emotions change. They also have cells in their skin and muscles. These cells make it possible for them to expand to make their color lighter; they can also contract their bodies to make the colors brighter or duller. They have the ability to produce different patterns of stripes and dots over their bodies as well. In this way, they can communicate with enemies, rivals, and mates. For example, a male octopus turns red when it is frightened, angry, or if it sees a female.

16. **B. Jet propulsion.** Scallops live on the seabed. One of their main predators is the starfish. Scallops are able to look out for these predators by using dozens of bright-blue eyes on the edges of their shells. When a scallop sees a starfish or any other predator approaching, it snaps its shell quickly. This makes the scallop shoot backwards away from its enemy.

17. **C. Both male and female.** After they mate, they both lay eggs.

18. **A. An edible sea snail.**

Ocean Creatures: Mollusks—Answers (cont.)

19. **B. Eat their arms off.** Sometimes a predator will also bite off an arm and, as in many species, another arm will grow in its place. The new arm is usually smaller than the original.

20. **B. Changes from male to female.**

21. **D. Sex.**

22. **A. One minute.** In four months, it is it possible for it to lay 400 million eggs

23. **C. Shooting darts at each other.** The darts are small and are made of a chalk-like substance.

24. **B. It impersonates other sea creatures.** There are a lot of animals that are able to change their colors to match their surroundings, so they cannot be detected by their enemies. Others pretend they are other animals that may be more ferocious or that may not taste good. However, the mimic octopus goes one step further. It is able to impersonate one animal and then switch to impersonate another. It can impersonate a sea snake, a sole fish, a lionfish, and others. It not only changes its colors to look like these fish, it changes the shape of its body and modifies its swimming to match those creatures. All of the creatures the octopus imitates are poisonous. Scientists believe that the mimic octopus also decides which imitation to do based on the predator that is close by. In other words, when a predator comes close, the mimic will impersonate a predator of that creature.

25. **C. Snorkels.** Apple snails live in swamps with little oxygen, so they extend a long tube up to the surface in order to breathe. This tube acts the same way as a snorkel tube. Apple snails are popular aquarium pets.

26. **B. Starves herself to death.** Once males and females pair off and mate, they do not mate with any other partners. After mating, the female attaches strands of eggs to the ceiling of her den. The common octopus, *Octopus vulgaris*, may lay 200,000–400,000 eggs. The female octopus will continually work to keep the algae and bacteria from growing on the eggs. She makes sure they have enough oxygen by squirting them with water. When the eggs are ready to hatch, the female helps the baby octopuses break loose from the egg case. Only one or two out of 200,000 eggs will survive to become an adult octopus. Most females will not eat after laying eggs. The female is intent on protecting her brood and will stay with her eggs instead of looking for food. She will die shortly after her eggs have hatched, but the male will stay with her. It does not mate again.

27. **C. Becoming transparent.** When a predator is near, a squid can become transparent so its enemies can see right through it. If that doesn't work, it will turn dark in an attempt to scare the predator away. If this doesn't work, the squid will eject a cloud of ink and then quickly swim away.

28. **A. Fly.** Flying squids live in tropical and temperate waters. They stay deep in the water and come up to the surface to feed at night. Near the surface, they are at risk for being eaten by tuna, sharks, and dolphins, so they fly away from these predators by using jet propulsion. A flying squid will take water into its mantle cavity and squirt the water out at a high pressure through a siphon on its underside. The squid can reach speeds of 20 miles per hour and can leave the water. Using its lateral "wings," it can glide for several yards. Once in the air, however, it is not safe. It may be eaten by a large bird, such as an albatross.

Name: _____ Date: _____

Ocean Creatures: Crustaceans

Crustaceans belong to the group of animals called **Arthropoda**. This is the largest group in the animal kingdom, which includes spiders, insects, centipedes, millipedes, lobsters, crabs, shrimp, barnacles, and wood lice. It is estimated that 84 percent of the known animal species are members of this **phylum**. Crustaceans usually live in water. While arthropods differ widely in appearance, habits, and habitats, they all have an exoskeleton covering their bodies. An **exoskeleton** is a rigid, shell-like covering that protects and supports the soft tissue of the animal. An exoskeleton does not grow with the animal and is regularly molted (shed), and then a new one is grown. The body of an arthropod is usually composed of segments.

1. The boxer crab got its name because:
   A. It punches its enemy in the face.
   C. Its shell opens like a box.
   B. It is shaped like a box.
   D. It lives near Box, England.

2. The hermit crab:
   A. Lives in a cave.
   C. Lives in a borrowed shell.
   B. Stays by itself.
   D. Lives in a tree.

3. The robber crab is unusual because it:
   A. Lives in fresh water.
   C. Climbs trees.
   B. Lives in Antarctica.
   D. Wears a mask of seaweed.

4. When attacked, the Acanthephyra shrimp surprises its enemy by:
   A. Spinning.
   C. Turning inside out.
   B. Attacking the predator.
   D. Vomiting glowing goop in its face.

5. What interests scientists about the barnacle?
   A. Its shell   B. Its poison   C. Its glue   D. Its flesh

6. Lobsters' blood is:
   A. Red   B. White   C. Blue   D. Striped

7. For every 25,000 eggs from a female lobster, how many survive?
   A. 2,000   B. 200   C. 20   D. 2

8. The crayfish's liver is:
   A. In its head.   B. In its stomach.   C. In its tail.   D. In its nose.

9. In colonial times, lobsters were fed only to:
   A. Men.   B. Women.   C. Aristocrats.   D. Slaves.

10. Lobsters are most closely related to:
    A. Clams.   B. Sharks.   C. Spiders.   D. Crocodiles.

Name: _____ Date: _____

Ocean Creatures: Crustaceans (cont.)

11. The sponge crab:
    A. Sometimes wears flip-flops.
    B. Is used to wash dishes.
    C. Can hold one gallon of water.
    D. Can eat 100 sponges a day.

12. The *Artema nyos,* a relative of the brine shrimp, is sometimes called:
    A. A salt shrimp.   B. A saline shrimp.   C. A sea monkey.   D. A prawn.

13. If shrimp and lobsters are kept in a tank without sand for a long period of time, they will eventually:
    A. Die.
    B. Stand on their heads.
    C. Change colors.
    D. Stop eating.

14. During the Middle Ages, people thought that gooseneck barnacles were:
    A. Developing geese.
    B. Whales' eyes.
    C. Octopus eggs.
    D. A cure for tuberculosis.

15. Some species of the hermit crab protect themselves with:
    A. Poison tentacles.
    B. Making shadows with their pincers.
    C. Bodyguards.
    D. Pistol shrimp.

16. The pistol shrimp received its name because:
    A. It makes the sound of a gunshot.
    B. It is shaped like a pistol.
    C. It is shaped like a bullet.
    D. The outline of a pistol is on its shell.

17. Before a female fiddler crab chooses a mate, she:
    A. Expects a gift.
    B. Inspects the prospective mate's home.
    C. Prepares a breeding burrow.
    D. Throws a shower.

18. Which color of lobster does not turn red when cooked?
    A. Yellow   B. Blue   C. White   D. Red

19. How does a lobster breathe?
    A. Through its mouth
    B. Through its head
    C. Through its legs
    D. Through its gills

20. A lobster "smells" its food by using its:
    A. Mouth.   B. Antennae.   C. Feet.   D. Nose.

21. Lobsters come in many colors. A blue lobster is born one in _____ times.
    A. 2,000   B. 200,000   C. 2,000,000   D. 2,000,000,000

35

Ocean Creatures: Crustaceans—Answers

1. **A. It punches its enemy in the face.** Ordinarily, a punch from a crab would have little effect, but the boxer crab has a secret weapon. It has "boxing gloves" that sting its enemy. The boxing gloves are actually anemones, which the crab has enticed to sit on its front pincers. Anemones are small sea animals that have stinging cells in their tentacles, which they use to paralyze their prey. So when an enemy gets too close, the boxer crab punches it in the face. It will also use this secret weapon to get food.

2. **C. Lives in a borrowed shell.** The hermit crab does not have a shell of its own, so in order to protect itself, it needs to find an abandoned shell and make its home in it. If it finds an empty shell that looks about the right size, it will inspect it carefully. If it passes inspection, it will clean out any litter or rubbish and climb in to see if the shell fits. If it is satisfactory, the crab will climb in and seal the opening with its large pincer. Since the shell it has chosen is too small for two large pincers, the hermit crab has developed only one large pincer, which is used to guard the entrance. The other pincer is much smaller. When the crab grows too large for the shell, it moves out and finds a new one that fits. Why is this creature called a hermit crab? Many years ago, holy men would go into the desert and live alone in order to serve God. They often lived in a cave or in a small house by themselves, much like the hermit crab in its shell; they were called "hermits."

3. **C. Climbs trees.** There are many species of crabs that make their home on land. Some can climb trees. One of the best-known is named the robber crab, also sometimes called the coconut crab. Using the pointed tips on its legs, this native of the islands in the Indian Ocean and southwestern Pacific climbs trees to find food or to get away from the heat or predators. These relatives of the hermit crab live in sand burrows but come out at night when it is cool in order to eat. They will eat the fruit of sago palms, other vegetation, and coconuts that have fallen onto the ground. They sometimes even eat carrion, which is the carcass of a dead animal.

4. **D. Vomiting glowing goop in its face.** While the octopus shoots a dark ink to confuse a predator in order to escape, the Acanthephyra shrimp does just the opposite. It vomits a shiny cloud of goop that is so bright, it momentarily blinds and confuses the enemy, giving the shrimp a chance to escape. Many sea creatures are luminous (glowing). Many of the types of seafood humans eat are luminous, but may not be noticed in a brightly lit store or restaurant. This glowing effect is sometimes seen when one is eating by candlelight. If a person is not familiar with this glowing quality, it may look as if something is wrong with the food.

5. **C. Its glue.** Barnacles look like mollusks because they have a shell-like covering, but barnacles are really crustaceans, closely related to lobsters, shrimp, and crabs. When they are larvae, they look like small shrimp. When they are older, they find a spot to which they attach themselves. It can be a ship's hull, rocks, pilings, driftwood, or even large sea creatures, such as whales. The barnacle then secures itself headfirst to the surface with a glue it secretes. The glue is so strong, the barnacle cannot be removed. It is stronger than epoxy cement. Just a very small amount of this glue can support 7,000 pounds. It will not soften until the temperature reaches 6,000°F; it will not melt.

Ocean Creatures: Crustaceans—Answers

Humans have not discovered any substance to dissolve this amazing glue. If humans could discover the secret of this glue and learn how to manufacture it, it would have hundreds of uses. Buildings could be assembled without nails or rivets. Doctors could use it to mend broken bones, and dentists would be able to permanently secure fillings or crowns.

6. **C. Blue.** A lobster's blood has no color until it is exposed to oxygen, and then it becomes blue.

7. **D. 2.** A newly laid lobster egg is only the size of the head of a pin. The number of eggs a female carries depends on her size. A one-pound female lobster will carry about 8,000 eggs inside her for nine to twelve months. Then, for the next nine to twelve months, she will carry the **swimmerets** outside her body under her tail. When the eggs hatch, the small larvae float near the surface of the water for four to six weeks. They are very vulnerable at this time, and few survive. Those that do will settle to the bottom and develop into baby lobsters. It will take them five to seven years to weigh one pound. This is considered the legal size for lobster fishermen to catch them.

8. **A. In its head.** Its teeth are in its stomach.

9. **D. Slaves.** Lobsters were so plentiful in New England during the colonial period that they were used primarily as fertilizer for crops or for bait to catch fish. Lobster was considered a food that only the poor should eat, so indentured servants and slaves were fed lobsters at most meals. Children and livestock were also given lobsters to eat. During the seventeenth century, when indentured servants were brought to this country, they would stipulate that they were not to be fed lobster more than three times a week.

10. **C. Spiders.** Lobsters and other crustaceans, such as crayfish, crabs, shrimp, and barnacles, are similar to spiders, insects, and other arthropods.

11. **A. Sometimes wears flip-flops.** The sponge crab is sometimes called the sleepy crab or little hairy crab. It received its name "sponge crab" because of its habit of removing a piece of living sponge and shaping it to fit its shell. The crab will carry the living sponge on its back by holding it on with its last two pairs of legs. The sponge acts as camouflage to protect it from predators. If a sponge is not available, a sponge crab has been known to use lost or discarded flip-flops on its back.

12. **C. A sea monkey.** When a man named Harold von Braunhut noticed that a relative of brine shrimp, which appeared to be dead, would come back to life when put in water, he began to sell them through the mail as "sea monkeys." Millions of these shrimp have been sold through the mail, and children have raised them in aquariums. Their ability to "appear dead" is their method of surviving when their salt lake dries up. The shrimp are able go into a state where they use no energy and give the impression they are dead. When the rains come and the lakes fill back up, the shrimp comes back to life. Its relative, the brine shrimp, uses a similar method to survive. They lay two kinds of eggs. Some have thin shells, while others have thick shells. Those with thin shells hatch right away, but those with thick shells sink into the mud. If the lake dries up, all of the brine shrimp will die, but the eggs with the thick shells remain. They can stay alive for up to

Ocean Creatures: Crustaceans—Answers (cont.)

five years. Strong winds blowing over the dried-up lake bed will blow many of these eggs, which are quite small, into the air. Many will fall to the ground and never hatch, but others will fall into water and hatch. Those that remain in the lake bed may hatch when the rains return to fill the lake.

13. **B. Stand on their heads.** Both shrimp and lobster are able to sense gravity by the sand they store in boxes in the sides of their heads. So if either of these creatures is kept in a tank without sand and it molts (sheds its shell), it will not be able to fill the boxes with sand. Without sand, it will be unable to maintain its balance and will stand on its head.

14. **A. Developing geese.** People thought that when the barnacles grew large enough, they would fall into the water and become adult geese. This idea arose from the fact that geese would breed in the summer north of the Arctic Circle and then would live in northern Europe along the coasts in the summer. Since the adult geese seemed to arrive out of nowhere, people tried to explain it with a story of the geese coming from gooseneck barnacles. Some have suggested a different reason for believing that geese came from barnacles in the ocean. If geese came from the sea, then they were really fish and could be eaten on days when religion forbade the eating of meat.

15. **C. Bodyguards.** For added protection, some species of the hermit crab will entice a sea anemone to sit on the shell. The sting of an anemone is enough to keep many predators away. Occasionally when the crab outgrows its shell and moves into another, the anemone moves with it.

16. **A. It makes the sound of a gunshot.** This shrimp is also called the popping shrimp, click shrimp, and snapping shrimp. Even though the pistol shrimp are not very large, they can make a very loud click when they snap shut their large claws. The sound is so loud that some have described it as the sound of a gunshot. Some people keep these shrimp in aquariums, but they often wonder if they made the right decision when they hear the sound of gunshots in the middle of the night. Sometimes the pistol shrimp will form what some people call an alliance with the shrimp goby, a fish. The pistol shrimp will dig a hole for itself and for the shrimp goby in which they can hide if an enemy approaches. The pistol shrimp will also feed the goby. How does the goby repay these favors? Since it has better eyesight, it will inform the pistol shrimp when a predator approaches.

17. **B. Inspects the prospective mate's home.** Fiddler crabs received their name because the male holds one claw, which is always much larger than the other, up in the air like a violin. The male fiddler uses its large claw to wrestle other males, to attract females, and to mark its territory. The small claw is used to gather food. If the male loses its large claw, the small claw will develop into a large claw. The female has two small claws. During the breeding period, the male crab will build a mating burrow that it will defend from other males. Then the male will wait in front of its burrow for the

Ocean Creatures: Crustaceans—Answers (cont.)

females to return from foraging for food. As the females pass, the male tries to attract them by waving its overly large claw. If a female is attracted, she will stop and look at him, and the male will wave more enthusiastically. She will shop around and check out several males before showing an interest in one. When this happens, the male will run toward her and back to its burrow several times. Finally, she will follow the male to its burrow. She will spend a few minutes inside the burrow and then check out several other males and their burrows before she decides on one. When she chooses a mate, she will not leave the burrow, and the male blocks the burrow entrance with sand. After mating, the male leaves the burrow and plugs it up again. The male leaves, and the female incubates her eggs for two weeks.

18. **C. White.**
19. **C. Through its legs.** It takes in water through its legs and lets it out through its head.
20. **B. Antennae.** They also use the small sensing hairs that cover their bodies.
21. **C. 2,000,000.**

Name: _____   Date: _____

Collective Nouns for Birds

Some nouns refer to a single bird. Examples would include crow, eagle, or sparrow. There are other nouns that refer to a group of animals. These are called **collective nouns**. Examples would include a *herd*, *pack*, or *flock*. Many of these collective nouns are obvious and well known, while others are very unusual. Sometimes a group of birds is referred to by different collective nouns. A group of quail, for example, could be called either a *bevy* or *covey* of quail. Sometimes the group name changes because of the behavior of the birds. For example, geese are called a *flock* or *gaggle* when they are on the ground, but they are called a *skein* when in flight.

Directions: Listed below are a number of birds. At the bottom of the page are collective nouns for these birds. Write the collective noun in the blank opposite the bird to which it refers. One noun will be used twice.

1. Gulls _____
2. Jays _____
3. Crows _____
4. Cranes _____
5. Eagles _____
6. Hawks _____
7. Finches _____
8. Larks _____
9. Herons _____
10. Parrots _____
11. Owls _____
12. Peacocks _____
13. Penguins _____
14. Ravens _____

15. Woodpeckers _____
16. Woodcocks _____
17. Waterfowl _____
18. Storks _____
19. Sparrows _____
20. Turkeys _____
21. Buzzards _____
22. Cormorants _____
23. Nightingales _____
24. Turtledoves _____
25. Coots _____
26. Lapwings _____
27. Swans _____
28. Starlings _____

Use these words:

Bank	Cast	Charm	Colony	Company	Convocation	Cover
Deceit	Descent	Exaltation	Fall	Gulp	Herd	Host
Murder	Murmuration	Mustering	Ostentation	Parliament	Party	Pitying
Plump	Rafter	Siege	Unkindness	Wake	Watch	

Name: _____ Date: _____

Birds

Birds are warm-blooded vertebrates covered with feathers. They have hollow bones. Their forearms are shaped into wings.

1. Some birds use ants for:
   A. Insect repellent.
   C. Pets.
   B. Food.
   D. Slaves.

2. In order to entice a mate, the male bowerbird:
   A. Does aerial tricks.
   C. Brings her flowers.
   B. Paints its nest.
   D. Sings her an original song.

3. The rare golden-shouldered parrot makes its home:
   A. Under waterfalls.
   C. In termite mounds.
   B. In bat caves.
   D. In beehives.

4. In order to protect the female hornbill as she incubates her eggs, the male will:
   A. Build a jail and put her in it.
   C. Guard the nest without eating.
   B. Build a nest next to a hornet's nest.
   D. Build a nest on a cliff.

5. Swifts and swiftlets of Malaysia and Borneo make their nests of:
   A. Hair.   B. Feathers.   C. Spit.   D. Spider webs.

6. The tailorbird was given its name because:
   A. It sews.
   C. Its mating call is, "tayyyyylor."
   B. It was discovered by Maynard Tailor.
   D. It looked like Zachary Taylor.

7. Owls hear so well because of their:
   A. Eyes.   B. Beak.   C. Face.   D. Sense of smell.

8. Vultures in Africa open ostriches' eggs by:
   A. Pecking at them.
   C. Dropping them from a great height.
   B. Throwing rocks at them.
   D. Tricking an animal to step on them.

9. In order to hunt, the African black heron:
   A. Uses small fish as bait.
   C. Dives under water.
   B. Turns itself into an umbrella.
   D. Follows a rhinoceros.

10. The color of a grouse's feathers is determined by:
    A. Its sex.   B. Its age.   C. The length of day.   D. The temperature.

11. The tawny frogmouth of Southeast Asia and Australia is rarely disturbed by predators when it is resting because it imitates a:
    A. Frog.   B. Broken stump.   C. Snake.   D. Koala bear.

Name: _____ Date: _____

 Birds (cont.)

12. The Australian lyrebird can be considered an entertainer because it:
    A.   Dances.
    B.   Has over a hundred different songs.
    C.   Does impressions
    D.   Juggles.

13. The emperor penguin travels quickly over the snow and ice by:
    A.   Running.
    B.   Skating.
    C.   Tobogganing.
    D.   Flying.

14. Cormorants hunt:
    A.   Underwater.
    B.   With their eyes closed.
    C.   In pairs.
    D.   With a spear.

15. Hummingbirds' wings can flap as fast as:
    A.   10 beats per second.
    B.   50 beats per second.
    C.   100 beats per second.
    D.   200 beats per second.

16. The bird that migrates the longest distance is the:
    A.   Canadian goose.
    B.   Arctic tern.
    C.   Hummingbird.
    D.   Albatross.

17. Canaries decide how hungry a chick is by the:
    A.   Size of its mouth.
    B.   Size of its eyes.
    C.   Color of its mouth.
    D.   Sound of its chirps.

18. The ringed plover protects its nest by:
    A.   Acting.
    B.   Puffing itself up to look larger.
    C.   Attacking with its talons.
    D.   Camouflage.

19. The little auk, or dovekie, found in the Arctic and North Atlantic Ocean,:
    A.   Flies in the air.
    B.   Flies underwater.
    C.   Flies both in the air and underwater.
    D.   Cannot fly.

20. A sand grouse has a built-in:
    A.   Hearing aid.
    B.   Pair of stilts.
    C.   Stopwatch.
    D.   Sponge.

21. Birds often fly in a "V" formation:
    A.   Because it looks cool.
    B.   For protection.
    C.   To better navigate.
    D.   To save energy.

22. The emperor penguin is able to dive so deep and fast because it:
    A.   Swallows stones.
    B.   Is very heavy.
    C.   Is shaped like a torpedo.
    D.   Has so much body fat.

23. When attacked, the petrel, a giant bird of the Antarctic, defends itself by:
    A.   Screeching loudly.
    B.   Pretending to die.
    C.   Vomiting in its attacker's face.
    D.   Head-butting its attacker.

Name: _____ Date: _____

Birds (cont.)

24. The male finfoot carries its chicks:
    A. In its pocket.   B. Under its wing.   C. On its back.   D. In its talons.

25. Who has the most neck bones?
    A. Humans   B. Giraffes   C. Ducks   D. Swans

26. The swallows traditionally return to San Juan Capistrano, California, on March 19. What birds return to Hinckley, Ohio, on March 15?
    A. Sparrows   B. Buzzards   C. Bluebirds   D. Geese

27. The female knot-tying weaverbird will refuse to mate with a male that:
    A. Is not colorful enough.   B. Builds a shoddy nest.
    C. Is too small.   D. Does not sing well.

28. In Southern California, in order to find gas leaks, utility workers use:
    A. Canaries.   B. Turkey buzzards.
    C. Roadrunners.   D. Acme gas detectors.

29. In order to light their nests, the baya birds of India:
    A. Build their nests in streetlights.   B. Paint their nests white.
    C. Add lightning bugs to their nests.   D. Line their nests with aluminum foil.

30. How does a peacock give birth?
    A. Lays eggs   B. Live chicks   C. Both A and B   D. Neither A nor B.

31. Flamingoes eat:
    A. Upside-down   B. Only after dark.
    C. Only water lilies.   D. Crocodile eggs.

32. Penguins have an organ above their eyes that:
    A. Converts seawater to freshwater.   B. Enables them to see in the dark.
    C. Filters out ultraviolet rays.   D. Allows them to see underwater.

33. The dipper, a wren, hunts for food:
    A. By walking underwater.   B. By walking on the water.
    C. In groups of three.   D. Only with its mate.

34. Kookaburras are known as the _____ of Australia.
    A. Fisher kings   B. Treetop roosters
    C. Laughing jackasses   D. Snake-eaters

35. Cassowaries are birds that:
    A. Kill crocodiles.   B. Can fly to South America.
    C. Are about $6\frac{1}{2}$ feet tall.   D. Are the size of a bee.

Birds—Answers

1. **A. Insect repellent.** Ants contain a chemical called formic acid, which some birds have discovered can act as a disinfectant to repel parasites. The bird will grasp the ant in its bill and rub the insect along its feathers. When the ant is disturbed, it squirts the formic acid from its abdomen, so the chemical is distributed over the bird's body. Scientists call this procedure "anting."

2. **B. Paints its nest.** When it is time to mate, the male bowerbird will build and decorate a special nest. It decorates the nest with flowers, feathers, berries, and any brightly colored bit of material it can find. After all of the decorating is finished, it will find a blueberry, press the juice out with its beak, and then using a piece of bark for a brush, it will paint the whole nest. After mating, this nest is abandoned, and a new one is built for raising the young.

3. **C. In termite mounds.** The golden-shouldered parrot lives in northern Queensland, Australia, where it nests in termite mounds.

4. **A. Build a jail and put her in it.** The female hornbill finds a hole in a tree for nesting. While she sits on the eggs, the male mixes mud with saliva and transports it to the nest. The pair then builds a wall of mud in the front of the hole. When the mud dries, it becomes hard and provides protection for the nesting female.

5. **C. Spit.** Unlike other birds who have to search and carry materials to build their nests, swifts and swiftlets use their own spit to build their white nests. During the breeding season, the swiftlet's throat becomes larger, making it possible for the bird to make large quantities of saliva. It chooses a spot on a ledge to nest and then dabs that spot with saliva, which quickly hardens. It continues the process for several days until it has built a nest large enough to hold two eggs. The nests are considered a delicacy and are served in fine restaurants in Southeast Asia.

6. **A. It sews.** The tailorbird is a native of India and other parts of Asia. It uses spider's silk, hair, and other materials to stitch together leaves for its nest. The female will pull two leaves together that are hanging close to each other, peck holes in them, and then, using the silk, will sew them together. She will pull them tight and then tie a knot to hold them securely. After a few days, there will be a nest of leaves. The nest will provide a camouflage for the bird's eggs and young.

7. **C. Face.** Although a barn owl's ears are below its feathers, it has an amazing ability to hear. Part of an owl's ability to hear so well comes from the design of its face. The tightly packed feathers, shaped like a heart, collect the sounds and concentrate them towards the owl's ears. Owls hunt at night and have good night vision, but their ability to hear the slightest sound enables them to be successful hunters.

8. **B. Throwing rocks at them.** Ostrich eggs provide a huge, delicious meal for African vultures. The problem for the vultures, however, is how to break the strong shell protecting this potential meal. The egg is too large for the vulture to pick up and drop, so it throws rocks at it. It will pick up a smooth stone and throw it at the egg. It may have to repeat the process many times until it is finally successful.

9. **B. Turns itself into an umbrella.** The heron will stand in shallow water, put its wings above its back, and put the tips of its wings down, so they barely touch the surface of the water. Then the bird will tuck its head under these outstretched wings and look at the water below. The shade under the wings makes it easier to see the fish. At the

Birds—Answers

same time, the fish believes this large shadow is vegetation or a rock that will provide it shelter. When the unsuspecting fish gets close by, the heron will stab it with its long beak.

10. **C. The length of day.** For protection from its predators, the willow grouse has brown feathers in the summer and white feathers in winter. In the Arctic Circle, where the willow grouse lives, the long summer days become shorter, and this activates the grouse's hormones, causing it to lose the brown plumage it has had all summer long. It slowly becomes white and is more difficult to see when it snows. Then in the spring when the days begin to lengthen, it changes color again and becomes brown.

11. **B. Broken stump.** The tawny frogmouth of Southeast Asia and Australia has an enormous, wide, frog-like mouth, which is used to capture insects. It has short legs and a large, hooked bill. With its eyes closed and its head up, its color and shape make it look like the stump of a tree.

12. **C. Does impressions.** Found in Australia, lyrebirds are shy birds that have an amazing talent. They are able to mimic the calls of other birds and other noises. Birdwatchers are often fooled into thinking they are stalking several species of birds, only to learn they are trailing a single lyrebird. Lyrebirds can also imitate chainsaws, barking dogs, and the sounds of cars.

13. **C. Tobogganing.** Penguins are excellent swimmers, but on land, their short legs make it difficult for them to travel fast or far. But certain species of penguin have devised a way to move quickly over the snow and ice. They flop down on their bellies and use their feet and wings to move, like a toboggan. They are not only able to cover great distances by tobogganing, they use much less energy than if they walked.

14. **A. Underwater.** Cormorants are a family of fish eaters that live along freshwater and saltwater shores around the world. They are strong diving birds and are able to swim as deep as 180 feet and stay under the water for more than a minute. When under water, they hunt for fish, squid, and shrimp. Japanese fishermen use the cormorant's fishing skills to catch fish for themselves. Some Japanese fishermen keep cormorants as pets and take them along when they go fishing. The fisherman will tie a chain around the bird's neck so that it cannot swallow a fish, and then he will release the bird. The bird dives, catches a fish, and since it cannot swallow the fish because of the chain, it flies back to the boat where the fisherman takes the fish from the bird.

15. **D. 200 beats per second.** Hummingbirds are among the most acrobatic of all birds. They can fly forward, backward, sideways, upside-down, straight up or down, and even hover in one spot.

16. **B. Arctic tern.** Many birds are able to travel great distances. Albatross parents may fly over 9,000 miles in 24 hours over the southern oceans in order to find food for their young. Actually, the albatross glides most of the time rather than flapping its wings. It will fly day and night with only a few stops. While the albatross's long flights are impressive, the Arctic tern gets the prize for the bird who migrates the farthest. It literally flies from one end of the world to the other. It nests in the Arctic at the top of the world and then flies to the Antarctic at the bottom of the world each year. That is a round-trip flight of more than 25,000 miles. The Arctic tern spends eight months of the year migrating between the Arctic and the Antarctic. Other long-distance migrating birds include sanderlings

Birds—Answers (cont.)

and golden plovers that fly 12,400 miles between Canada and South America each year. Even the little rufous hummingbird flies 3,730 miles from the northwest coast of North America to Mexico each year.

17. **C. Color of its mouth.** When a canary chick is hungry, the inside of its mouth becomes bright red. Those chicks that are the hungriest have mouths that are bright red. Those that aren't quite as hungry may have mouths that are only pink. This helps parents decide who needs to be fed first when they fly to the nest and see all of the chicks with their mouths open, begging for food. There is a scientific reason for this phenomenon. If a chick has recently been fed and is digesting food, its blood supply travels towards its stomach, and so it has a lighter-colored mouth. Those chicks with empty stomachs have more blood available to make their mouths brighter.

18. **A. Acting.** The ringed plover builds its nest on the ground, making it vulnerable to predators. When a predator gets too close to the nest, the plover pretends to have a broken wing and makes a distressful cry. As the predator approaches, expecting to get an easy meal, the plover moves away from its nest. When the predator is far enough away from the nest, the plover flies away.

19. **C. Flies both in the air and underwater.** The little auk, or dovekie, has wings large enough for flying, yet small enough to propel it through water. In the air, its whirring flight is characterized by rapid wing beats, and it also flaps its wings to "fly" underwater. The auk, which is found in the Arctic and North Atlantic Ocean, resembles a tiny puffin. It pursues prey, such as tiny shrimp, under water, carrying them back to its chick in its throat pouch.

20. **D. Sponge.** Most birds live in areas close to water so that they can drink whenever they need to. However, the Namaqualand sand grouse of northwestern South Africa doesn't need to do this. This grouse may live over 180 miles from a water source and may fly there each day in order to drink and collect water to bring back to its nest for the chicks. Once by the water hole, the sand grouse will wade into the water and drink as much as it wants. While most of its feathers are water-repellent, the feathers on its chest absorb the water like a sponge. When it flies back to its nest, the chicks can drink the four teaspoons of water that is available in the feathers.

21. **D. To save energy.** The lead bird in the "V" formation works the hardest. It has to "break through" the air. The air behind the lead bird becomes turbulent, and this makes it easier to fly for those birds behind the leader. After a while, the lead bird will tire and fall back in the formation. Another bird that is not as tired will take over the lead. Recently, however, a team of French scientists has discovered another advantage of flying in a "V" formation. Not only do the birds benefit from the airstreams of the birds in front of them, but those behind are able to glide more often.

22. **A. Swallows stones.** The emperor penguin has small stones in its stomach that provide extra weight, enabling it to dive 70 feet underwater to catch fish and squid. It can stay underwater for 20 minutes. The emperor penguin is the largest of the many species of penguins. It lives in the cold Antarctic. There are no penguins at the North Pole or anywhere in the Northern Hemisphere. All species of penguin live below the equator.

Birds—Answers (cont.)

23. **C. Vomiting in its attacker's face.** It will either regurgitate food in its attacker's face or will squirt a jet of oil from its nostrils with a force that is so great, it can knock a person down.

24. **A. In its pocket.** Sometimes called sun grebes, the finfoot is found in parts of Asia, Africa, and Central and South America. The male finfoot has special pockets under its wings so it can carry its chicks when it flies. The finfoot is thought to be the only bird that carries its chicks in this way.

25. **D. Swans.** Humans and giraffes have seven neck bones, while ducks have 16, and swans have 23.

26. **B. Buzzards.**

27. **B. Builds a shoddy nest.** If the nest is not built to the female's satisfaction, the male will need to take the nest apart and rebuild it in order to be able to mate with the female.

28. **B. Turkey buzzards.** There are many turkey buzzards living in the desert of southern California. These birds have a very good sense of smell, so the utility company adds a substance to the gas that gives off an odor similar to an odor that excites the mating instincts of the buzzards. Whenever a utility lineman sees a cluster of turkey buzzards around a natural gas line, it usually means that there is a break in the line.

29. **C. Add lightning bugs to their nests.**

30. **D. Neither A nor B.** A peacock is male. The female, known as a peahen, lays eggs.

31. **A. Upside-down.** The flamingo prefers to eat mollusks. In order to do so, it turns its head upside-down so the bottom half of its beak faces the sky, and the top half of the beak is underwater. There are slits on the side of the top of its bill that filter out insects, weeds, sand, and other materials but holds in the mollusks. While some flamingoes in Africa feed on algae, they scoop up their food in the same way.

32. **A. Converts seawater to freshwater.**

33. **A. By walking underwater.** The dipper can close its nostrils when it dives, and its feathers are waterproofed. In order to look for food, it walks along the bottom of swiftly flowing steams and rivers. It is not a heavy bird, so it is a challenge not to be washed away by the water. It dives against the current, bows its head, and points its tail upward so that the flowing water pushes it down as it walks.

34. **C. Laughing jackasses.** The kookaburra is a bird related to the family of kingfishers. It has a stout body, short neck, short legs, and a pointed bill. What makes the kookaburra unique is its laugh. It is a loud, rolling laugh. Flocks of kookaburras emit a chorus of these bizarre, laughing calls at dusk and then again as soon as dawn breaks. Their calls are so regular that kookaburras are sometimes called the "bushman's clock." The kookaburra is invaluable as part of the ecological system because it eats snakes and lizards.

35. **C. Are about 6½ feet tall.** The cassowary is a very large bird that is unable to fly. It is found not only in Australia but in New Guinea as well. While it is the biggest bird in Australia, it is not the largest in the world. That honor goes to the ostrich. Cassowaries generally grow to be about 6½ feet tall and weigh about 130 pounds. However, the largest-known cassowary was 180 pounds—as large as an adult man. The female cassowary is even larger than the male.

Name: _____ Date: _____

Find the Birds

Directions: Several names of birds are hidden in these unusual sentences shown below. Find them by looking within words or between two or more words. Underline the names of the birds. Ignore punctuation marks. The first is given as an example.

1. The book of kn<u>ow</u>ledge can be read by anyone.
2. Apologies are important, though awkward.
3. Hippos prey on unsuspecting swimmers.
4. My dog is a beagle.
5. I am ravenous after that diet.
6. The child was given a balloon for her birthday.
7. Goo seeped out of the bag.
8. Listen to the birds coo tonight.
9. I do not regret my statement.
10. For breakfast, he enjoyed a flaming omelet.
11. The keys are either on the table or counter.
12. If you will hand me the scalpel, I can operate.
13. When she wore her jewelry, she felt very swanky.
14. Turn on the lantern, so that I can see.
15. Mac awakened suddenly.
16. Hand me the wrench, Bob.
17. Griffin charmed his enemies.
18. Clark slowly turned to see his attacker.
19. This is my native land.
20. Did you see these new micro binoculars?
21. The girl and boy both rushed to the ocean.
22. Don't be so gullible.
23. Ancient humans made mud huts to live in.
24. Would you like to ski with me?
25. I am not poor; I am almost rich.
26. She played a ukulele.
27. The emperor had a golden crown.
28. When you want to come in, buzz ardently.
29. The man craned his neck to watch his brother on the stage.
30. New York is an Eastern city.
31. San Francisco, Ottawa, and Santiago are all cities in the Americas.
32. "I do, do, do," shouted the bride.
33. Laminating your ID makes your card inalterably safe.
34. When I was a child, I read the gospel. I can read it again.

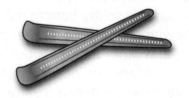

Name: _____ Date: _____

Reptiles: Alligators and Crocodiles

All of the species of crocodiles, alligators, caimans, and gharial are known together as **crocodilians**. Many people refer to all of the species in the group as "crocs." Crocodilians are reptiles and are cold-blooded animals. This means that their body temperature is controlled by the temperature around them. Crocs bask in the sun in order to regulate their body temperature. Since they are cold-blooded, their body rates slow down during the winter when it is cold, making it difficult for them to catch food. So they stay in holes underground and are dormant until the weather becomes warm again.

While the members of the species are similar in appearance, there are some differences. First, their natural habitats are different. Alligators are found in the southern United States and in eastern China. Caimans are found in Central and South America. Crocodiles are found in Mexico, Central America, South America, Africa, Australia, and Southeast Asia. Alligators, caimans, and crocodiles live in slow-moving rivers and swamps. Gharials are found in India in rivers with deep pools. A second way to tell the difference between an alligator and a crocodile is by their teeth. The fourth tooth on the lower jaw of crocodiles sticks up over the upper lip on crocodiles. This tooth is visible when the croc's mouth is closed. The same fourth tooth in alligators is covered. Another difference is the shape of the jaw. Crocodiles have long, pointed, V-shaped snouts. Alligators have wide, U-shaped, rounded snouts.

The American alligator is the largest reptile in North America. When the Spanish explorers came to the New World, they called this creature "El legarto" or "big lizard." Eventually, they became known as alligators. Most of the wild alligators in the United States are found in Louisiana and Florida. There are also many alligator farms.

1. The sex of a baby crocodile is determined by the:
   A. Mother.
   B. Father.
   C. Temperature.
   D. Season.

2. Crocodiles carry their young:
   A. On their tails.
   B. In their mouths.
   C. Under their arms.
   D. On a lily pad.

3. Crocodiles are intimidated by:
   A. Tall creatures.
   B. Snakes.
   C. Other reptiles.
   D. Mice.

4. The Nile crocodile cleans its teeth by:
   A. Eating reeds.
   B. Letting a bird clean them.
   C. Rinsing them with water.
   D. Chewing gravel.

Name: _____ Date: _____

Reptiles: Alligators and Crocodiles (cont.)

5. An alligator's strongest sense is:
    A. Sight.   B. Smell.
    C. Hearing.   D. Taste.

6. A newborn crocodile is:
    A. One-tenth the size of its egg. B. The same size as its egg.
    C. Three times larger than its egg. D. Ten times larger than its egg.

7. Can an alligator move faster on land or in the water?
    A. Faster on land than in water   B. Twice as fast in water than on land
    C. Three times faster in water   D. About as fast on land as in water

8. An alligator can go _____ without eating.
    A. One month   B. Six months
    C. One year   D. Six years

9. An alligator cannot breathe underwater. However, it is able to stay underwater and not take a breath for up to:
    A. One hour.   B. Two hours.
    C. Six hours.   D. Twenty-four hours.

10. If you are attacked by an alligator, your best defense is to:
    A. Run away in a straight line.   B. Run away in a zigzag pattern.
    C. Charge the alligator.   D. Stand still.

11. Crocodiles have been around longer than:
    A. Humans.   B. Dinosaurs.
    C. Africa.   D. Flowers.

Reptiles: Alligators and Crocodiles—Answers

1. **C. Temperature.** The sex of the embryos depends on the temperature at which the eggs were incubated during the first two to three weeks. If the nest temperature is 86°F or lower, the offspring will all be females. If the average nest temperature is 93°F or higher, then all of the offspring will be males. If the temperature falls between the two extremes, both female and male offspring will be produced.

2. **B. In their mouths.** When the young are hatched, the female carries them to the water in her mouth and then guards them for most of the first year of their lives. Sometimes the young crocs get to ride on her back. She will threaten or attack any predator that comes too close to her young, and in some species, she will call the hatchlings to swim into her mouth for protection. It will look as if she is eating them. The female gharial's mouth is too narrow for this purpose.

3. **A. Tall creatures.**

4. **B. Letting a bird clean them.** As a Nile crocodile cools, it may nap with its mouth open. Egyptian plovers, or crocodile birds, sometimes gather around the croc's mouth and eat insects, leeches, and meat from the croc's teeth and skin. This partnership between large animals and birds is not unique. A tickbird will ride on the back of the rhinoceros and eat ticks and other insects from the rhino's skin.

5. **C. Hearing.**

6. **C. Three times larger than its egg.**

7. **A. Faster on land than in water.**

8. **C. One year.** Crocs are very energy efficient. They are cold-blooded and use food mainly for growth, repair, and reproduction. As cold-blooded animals, they depend on external heat sources to regulate their body temperature, so they do not have to use food as energy to provide heat as humans and other warm-blooded mammals do. Crocodiles generally eat one meal a week. During the winter, they are not known to eat at all. Crocs do not chew their food, but swallow it whole.

9. **D. Twenty-four hours.** During cold weather, their hearts are designed to slow down and to divert blood away from the lungs while the animal is underwater.

10. **A. Run away in a straight line.** Alligators have a natural fear of people and aren't likely to attack humans. But if an alligator were to attack on land, there probably isn't much you could do because they do not usually chase their prey. Their hunting strategy is surprise, not speed. They lunge at their prey and capture it in a single movement. However, since alligators are territorial, it is possible that one may chase you away from its nest. So if you were attacked, you probably wouldn't have a chance to run. However, if there was a rare instance that an alligator did chase you, the best thing to do would be to run as fast as you could in a straight line. Alligators and crocodiles do not have the stamina to run very far on land. Some recommend running in a zigzag pattern, but there is no evidence that this is the best method. Others don't recommend running at all, but backing away slowly.

11. **A, B, C, D. All answers are correct.** Crocodiles have survived and, in fact, have changed very little over the countless centuries in which they have lived. They even survived the global catastrophe that caused the mass extinction of the dinosaurs and many other animal species. Giant crocodiles that were 45 to 60 feet long roamed the Big Bend area of West Texas. Their teeth were six inches long.

51

Name: _____ Date: _____

Reptiles: Lizards

Lizards are small reptiles. They are cold-blooded and have eyelids, long tails, and usu-ally four legs. While scientists have identified about 2,500 different species of lizards, only two species are poisonous. Lizards vary greatly in size. Some are less than three inches long, while the Komodo dragon is over 10 feet long.

1. The tuatara lizard is unusual because it:
   A. Doesn't have legs.
   B. Has three eyes.
   C. Is bright orange with purple spots.
   D. Does not need water to live.

2. Which of the following statements about the glass snake is *not* true?
   A. It is really a lizard.
   B. It is transparent.
   C. Its tail easily breaks into pieces.
   D. It can regrow a new tail.

3. When the male Anolis lizard from South and Central America is ready to mate, it:
   A. Sings a song.
   B. Flies a flag.
   C. Dances.
   D. Starts going out on dates.

4. The horned lizard has an unusual defense in that it:
   A. Spits blood from its eye.
   B. Uses karate.
   C. Flies away.
   D. Feeds the predator its children.

5. Geckos are the only lizards that have:
   A. Three eyes.
   B. A tail that can regrow.
   C. A voice.
   D. Live babies.

6. A chameleon:
   A. Has a short tail.
   B. Moves very quickly.
   C. Matches the colors of its surroundings.
   D. Lives underground.

Reptiles: Lizards— Answers

1. **B. Has three eyes.** The tuatara lizard of New Zealand is one of the oldest species on Earth. It is sometimes referred to as a living fossil because it looks exactly as it did when it first appeared on Earth. It has three eyes. Two eyes are in the center of its head, and there is an extra eye on the top of its head. Scientists aren't sure what the third eye is for, but many think it may help the lizard with directions because it can keep track of the sun. It may also help them keep track of time. Tuataras live in burrows separate from each other. While they sometimes dig their own burrows, they often move into a bird's burrow, such as that of a petrel, prion, or shearwater. Rather than moving, the birds will sometimes share their homes with a tuatara. This is not wise because a tuatara will eat eggs and chicks. However, most of the time, it will spare those in its own home and raid a neighbor's burrow.

2. **B. It is transparent.** The common name for a legless lizard that looks like a snake is the glass snake. Its body is gray or greenish-brown and sometimes striped. The American species grows to two or three feet in length, two-thirds of which is the tail. When struck, the tail of a glass snake breaks from its body and may break into several pieces. The lizard is able to regenerate (regrow) a new, usually shorter tail. Losing a tail is not unique to this specific lizard. Most lizards have this ability. When they are in danger, they can shed their tails. While the predator is occupied with the tail, the lizard is able to escape. The lizard can then grow a new tail that is almost as good as the original one, but this one cannot be shed.

3. **B. Flies a flag.** The Anolis lizards (anoles) have an unusual way of declaring that they are ready to mate. They develop large, brightly colored flags, called dewlaps, that hang below their throats. They display these flags and shake them at rivals. Some males are able to inflate the flags.

4. **A. Spits blood from its eye.** The horned lizard is sometimes called the horny toad. It has a short, rough-skinned body that looks more like a toad's body than a lizard's. It avoids predators by flattening against the ground. When confronted, however, it is able to spit blood out of its eye at the predator. It does this by restricting the flow of blood from its head, which bursts the small blood vessels in its eye membranes and causes blood to shoot out of its eye at the attacker. If this doesn't work, the large spines sticking out of the back of the lizard's head make it undesirable to eat.

5. **C. A voice.** Some species of geckos make a sound that sounds like "gecko."

6. **C. Matches the colors of its surroundings.** There are two groups of lizards commonly called "chameleons." Both can change color, but the kind found in Africa and Madagascar changes color mainly to communicate to other members of its species. The other group of chameleons are really **anoles**. These lizards are found in the southeastern United States, the Caribbean, and Central and South America and are closely related to iguanas. Not all anoles change color, but those that do only change between shades of brown and green for protection. This kind of "chameleon" changes its body color to match its background. When resting on a green leaf, it will turn green, but if it climbs onto a brown limb, it will turn brown. It does this to protect itself from predators. They cannot match any color background, as is commonly believed. A blind chameleon is still able to take on the colors of its environment.

Name: _____ Date: _____

Reptiles: Snakes and Turtles

Snakes are long reptiles without arms or legs. There are about 2,700 species of snakes, only a small number of which are venomous. Snakes come in all sizes. The largest is the anaconda, which can be 38 feet long; the smallest is the Brahminy blind snake, which is only two inches long. The body shape of a species of snake is determined, for the most part, by where it lives. Snakes that burrow in the ground are compact, while those that live in trees are long and thin. Snakes that live in the water tend to be flat. The colors of snakes also vary widely. Some have developed colors that help them blend into their environments so they are protected from predators. This also allows them to go unnoticed by the animals upon which they prey. Others, mainly venomous snakes, are brightly colored. Scientists believe that these bright colors act as a warning to predators that the snake is dangerous.

Turtles, tortoises, and terrapins are reptiles and are similar to each other but have different names. The different names are used to refer to the locations where the reptiles live and how they use their habitats. Turtles tend to have webbed feet for swimming because they spend most of their time in the water. Sea turtles rarely leave the ocean, except to come ashore to lay their eggs. Other turtles live in fresh ponds and lakes. They swim, but also climb out onto banks or logs to bask in the sun. On the other hand, tortoises do not have webbed feet because they live on land. Terrapins spend time both on land and in water, but always live near water. Turtles are also referred to differently in other parts of the world. In Australia, for example, only sea turtles are called turtles. Everything else is referred to as a tortoise.

1. There is a cobra in Africa that defends itself by:
   A. Blinding its attacker.
   B. Biting its attacker.
   C. Crushing its attacker.
   D. All of the above.

2. Flying snakes of Southeast Asia:
   A. Fly.
   B. Parachute.
   C. Only eat flies.
   D. Glide.

3. The number of segments in a rattlesnake's rattle is equal to:
   A. The snake's age.
   B. How often the skin has been shed.
   C. The number of times it has mated.
   D. The number of season changes.

4. How do snakes smell?
   A. With their noses
   B. With their tongues
   C. With their noses and tongues
   D. Terrible

Name: _____ Date: _____

Reptiles: Snakes and Turtles

5. Police have been known to use snapping turtles to help them:
   A. Detect drugs.
   B. Check for underwater explosives.
   C. Identify criminals.
   D. Find dead human bodies.

6. Snake charmers "charm" cobras with:
   A. Music.
   B. Hypnotic stares.
   C. Movement
   D. Food.

7. Snakes inhabit which one of the following locations?
   A. Ireland
   B. New Zealand
   C. Australia
   D. Antarctica

8. The sex of turtles is determined by:
   A. The food eaten by the parents.
   B. The amount of salt in the water.
   C. The temperature.
   D. The season.

9. Each year, more people are killed by:
   A. Bees.
   B. Bears.
   C. Snakes.
   D. Sharks.

10. Garter snakes are unusual reptiles because they:
    A. Avoid the sun.
    B. Are not cold-blooded.
    C. Bear live young.
    D. Are vegetarians.

Reptiles: Snakes and Turtles—Answers

1. **A. Blinding its attacker.** When the spitting cobra of Africa is threatened, it rises up, spreads its hood to warn its attacker, and then shoots venom from a tiny hole near the tip of each fang. The venom is so strong that if it hits the victim's eyes, it is very painful and can cause blindness. The venom can be sprayed over a distance of eight feet.

2. **B. Parachute.** Snakes don't fly because they don't have wings. But there are five different species of snake that are called "flying" snakes. Most are about three to four feet long and live in trees in the lowland tropical rain forests of Southeast and South Asia. While some people think that flying snakes "glide," they really "parachute." The flying snake is able to pull in its belly and form a U-shaped half-cylinder along its entire length. This concave surface acts like a parachute by increasing air resistance. At the same time, the snake moves like it is swimming in order to control its flight. Traveling in this way allows it to move over long distances quickly to escape predators or to catch prey.

3. **B. How often the skin has been shed.** Many people believe that one can tell a rattlesnake's age by counting its rattles. This is not true. While it is a fact that the more segments of rattles a snake has, the older it is, it does not produce a new rattle for each year of life. A rattlesnake adds a rattle segment every time it sheds. Young snakes may shed up to four times a year. In addition, segments sometimes fall off as the snake gets older.

4. **C. With their noses and tongues.** Being able to distinguish between different types of odors is critical for most species, including snakes. Odor detection is needed in order to find food and mates, avoid predators, and for other important activities. Snakes are able to taste the air with their tongues. When the tongue is extended, odor particles stick to it. When the tongue comes back into its mouth, the odor particles are transferred to the **Jacobson's organ**, which sends it to the brain to interpret. This unique method of odor detection enables the snake to avoid predators and track prey in total darkness. Snakes are also able to smell through their noses. Odors are sniffed or breathed in through the nasal passages and into the olfactory chambers.

5. **D. Find dead human bodies.** The snapping turtle, or snapper, will attack anything that comes close to it, including humans. It has a beak so sharp it can bite through a man's hand. Snapping turtles are **omnivorous**, which means they will eat almost anything. This includes aquatic creatures and plants. They don't have teeth, but they have very powerful jaws. They also eat carrion, which is the dead body of an animal. They have a well-developed ability to detect rotting flesh. In fact, the police have used snapping turtles to help them find dead human bodies that have not yet come to the surface of a lake. The police would tie the turtle to a rope and then release it into the water. When the turtle stopped, the police assumed it had found the body, and a diver would be sent into the water, or the police would drag the area with a hook.

6. **C. Movement.** "Snake charmers" are exciting to watch. A man in a turban will put a basket down and begin playing a bamboo instrument, similar to a flute. Almost immediately, a cobra will rise out of the basket and look around. It soon seems to be hypnotized by the music and stares at the charmer. It raises one-third of its body off the ground, flattens its neck into a menacing shape, and begins to sway back and forth. From time to time, the cobra lashes out at the snake charmer but misses him by inches. However, appearances can be deceiving. Since the snake does not have external ears, it does not hear

56

Reptiles: Snakes and Turtles—Answers (cont.)

the music of the snake charmer. While it does feel the vibration of the music, it most likely is not swaying to the music but following the movements of the snake charmer and the flute. The snake charmer is usually not in as much danger as it appears. Some snakes are not poisonous. Others have had their poison glands removed. Some even have had their mouths sewn shut. Since a cobra can only strike about one-third of its body length, which is its height when it is erect, the charmer knows how far to sit back from the basket. In addition, the cobra is not striking at the snake charmer, but at the flute, which is closer. Even a snake's small brain soon learns that striking a hard object like the flute is painful and futile. So after a while its lunge stops just short of the flute.

7. **C. Australia.** Snakes are found almost everywhere on Earth. They live in deserts, forests, and even oceans. However, there are no snakes living in Antarctica, Greenland, New Zealand, Iceland, or Ireland. Snakes do not generally live in polar regions or in high mountains. Since snakes are "cold-blooded," and take on the temperature of their surroundings, they need to burrow into the ground for protection during the winter. If the winter is too cold or lasts too long, snakes cannot survive. That explains why there are no snakes in places where it is very cold. There are a few exceptions to this rule. The European adder can be found in the Arctic in Siberia. But most snake species would freeze solid in this climate and choose warmer areas for their homes.

   However, this does not explain why there are no snakes in Ireland or New Zealand. Legend has it that there were snakes in Ireland, but Saint Patrick drove them from Ireland—he charmed them into the sea. Scientists have another explanation. During the Ice Age, Ireland was buried under a deep sheet of ice. No snake could have survived this cold, icy climate, so any that had lived in Ireland would have died. Even after the glaciers receded, Ireland remained frozen for hundreds of years. When Ireland eventually warmed up, the cold water around the island made it impossible for snakes to get there. There are no snakes living in New Zealand because it had separated from Australia and Asia before snakes evolved.

8. **C. The temperature.** In most turtles, the sex of the offspring is determined by the temperature in which the fertilized egg develops. For example, snapping turtle eggs when exposed to cold or hot temperatures turn into females, while those exposed to moderate temperatures develop into males. In other turtle species, high temperatures lead to male development, and low temperatures lead to female development.

9. **A. Bees.**

10. **C. Bear live young.** Even though garter snakes are reptiles, they do not lay eggs. They bear live young just as mammals do. Like most reptiles, garters warm up by basking in the sun. Their diet consists of birds, aquatic invertebrates, and other types of prey.

Name: _____ Date: _____

Amphibians

An **amphibian** is an animal that usually lives the first part of its life in water and the second part on land. An amphibian usually begins life as an aquatic, water-breathing larva without arms and legs, called a tadpole. It then develops into an air-breathing adult that lives at least part of its life on land. This change is called **metamorphosis**. There are about 3,000 species of amphibians, which fall into three groups: 1) those without tails, such as frogs and toads; 2) those with tails, such as salamanders and newts; and 3) legless, burrowing animals called caecilians that live only in the tropics.

Like reptiles, amphibians are cold-blooded, but there are differences between reptiles and amphibians. Newborn reptiles are small versions of the adult, while most amphibians pass through a larval stage before developing an adult body. While in this larval stage, they are dependent on water and live like fish, breathing through gills.

1. The fire-bellied toad is able to:
   A. Walk on water.
   B. Listen with its lungs.
   C. Breathe fire.
   D. Fly.

2. A frog in West Africa, known as the Goliath frog, is:
   A. Six inches long.
   B. One foot long.
   C. Two and a half feet long.
   D. Four and a half feet long.

3. Which of the following methods of self-defense is not used by the South American frog *Physalaemus nattereri*?
   A. Turns its back on predator.
   B. Secretes an unpleasant substance.
   C. Pretends to be hurt.
   D. Puffs itself up.

4. When underwater, a frog:
   A. Holds it breath.
   B. Breathes through its gills.
   C. Breathes through its skin.
   D. Breathes through its ears.

5. A frog drinks water through its:
   A. Mouth.
   B. Ears.
   C. Nose.
   D. Skin.

6. The marsupial frog:
   A. Cannot hop.
   B. Has a pouch in which it carries its young.
   C. Hibernates in the summer
   D. Is a mammal.

Name: _____ Date: _____

Amphibians (cont.)

7. Wood frogs can be:
    A. Used to cure warts.
    B. Burned like logs.
    C. Used to catch mice.
    D. Frozen solid and revived.

8. A newt is able to:
    A. Die and come back to life.
    B. Go for a year without eating.
    C. Hibernate for years.
    D. Regrow almost every part of its body.

9. The natives of South and Central America use a frog as:
    A. A pet.
    B. A weatherman.
    C. A weapon.
    D. Bait.

10. Before the barometer was discovered, what did meteorologists use to predict air pressure changes?
    A. Salamanders
    B. Frogs
    C. Newts
    D. Toads

11. The paradoxical frog is most unusual because:
    A. The male gets pregnant.
    B. It is transparent.
    C. It is the smallest frog in the world.
    D. It gets smaller as it gets older.

12. The Australian frog named *Rheobatrachus silus*:
    A. Vomits its newborns from its mouth.
    B. Gives birth to live young.
    C. Can't swim.
    D. Eats tadpoles.

13. Which statement about the red flying frog of Sumatra is *not* true?
    A. It has parachutes on its feet.
    B. It lay its eggs in trees.
    C. It cannot hop or jump.
    D. It is colorful.

Amphibians—Answers

1. **B. Listen with its lungs.** Most frogs and toads have an internal middle ear that sends sound to the inner ear, connected to the brain. But the fire-bellied toad does not use this method to hear. In its case, the sound waves go through the toad's mouth and vibrate its lungs. The waves are then transmitted to the toad's inner ear. Scientists feel that this unusual method of hearing was developed so that early amphibians were able to hear sounds under water as well as on land

2. **C. Two and a half feet long.** The Goliath is the world's largest frog. It can weigh more than seven pounds. While its body can be more than a foot long, when measured with the back legs extended, it can be more than two and a half feet long. The eggs and tadpoles of Goliath frogs are about the same size as those of other frogs, but as the tadpoles mature, they grow to a mammoth size.

3. **C. Pretends to be hurt.** On its rump are markings that appear to be large eyes. When threatened, the frog turns its back and raises its legs. The predator is startled to see what appears to be a large, dangerous creature staring at it. If this doesn't stop the predator, the frog secretes an unpleasant substance from its glands. This leaves a terrible taste in the predator's mouth. It can also "puff" itself up so it looks larger than it actually is. Since some of its predators, such as snakes, do not chew but swallow their food whole, the frog looks too big to eat.

4. **C. Breathes through its skin.** When underwater, a frog is able to breathe through its skin. Its skin has small blood vessels that make this possible. When the frog is on land, it can use both its skin and lungs to breathe.

5. **D. Skin.** The frog does not drink as most other creatures do. It gets all of the moisture it needs by absorbing water through its skin.

6. **B. Has a pouch in which it carries its young.** *Marsupial* is a term used to describe a group of mammals that carry their young in pouches. The young are usually small and need the mother's protection until they are able to survive on their own. Some examples of marsupials are the kangaroo, koala, and opossum. The marsupial frog does the same thing. The big difference is that the frog is not a mammal but an amphibian. There are several species of marsupial frogs. The Australian marsupial frog is one of the most unusual. After the eggs have hatched in the soil, the male carries the tadpoles in slits on its hips until the tadpoles become frogs.

7. **D. Frozen solid and revived.** Wood frogs can be frozen, then thawed, and continue to live. They are able to survive being frozen by increasing the amount of glucose stored in their cell fluids. Glucose is produced in their livers and pumped to their vital organs. Glucose acts as antifreeze, lowering the freeze point. By preventing the cells from freezing on the inside, the cell membrane is not ruptured, and the frog survives temperatures that would kill other creatures.

   While they are frozen, wood frogs' hearts beat very slowly, and they breathe very little. They spend the winter in a partially frozen state. In the late winter when the temperature begins to warm, they thaw out and continue with their lives.

Amphibians—Answers

8. **D. Regrow almost every part of its body.** Among adult vertebrates, newts and salamanders are the champions of regeneration. An adult newt can regenerate most parts of its body including its tail, limbs, jaws, eyes, and even large parts of its heart. In the eighteenth century, an Italian naturalist cut off the leg of a newt 1,374 times. Each time, the animal regrew the leg.

9. **C. A weapon.** There are many frogs that are poisonous, but one of the most poisonous is sometimes called the poison arrow frog. The poison paralyzes the heart and the nervous system. If a predator swallows one of these frogs or even licks it, it is deadly. The South and Central American natives would roast the frog until the poison dripped out. Then they would dip their arrows in the poison. The poison from one frog was enough for forty darts.

10. **B. Frogs.** Frogs croak when the barometric pressure drops.

11. **D. It gets smaller as it gets older.** When the paradoxical frog is a tadpole, it is between seven and ten inches in length. When it becomes an adult, it shrinks to two inches or less in length.

12. **A. Vomits its newborns from its mouth.** The female frog swallows the fertilized eggs, and they incubate inside the female's stomach. For the 6–7 weeks it takes for them to develop, she does not eat. Once they are fully developed, she vomits the tadpoles out of her mouth.

13. **C. It cannot hop or jump.** The red flying frog of Sumatra is colorful and a great jumper. When the female is ready to lay eggs, she climbs a tree and clings to a branch that is located over a puddle or pool. She lays a mass of foamy eggs on the branch; eventually the eggs hatch, and the tadpoles fall to the pool below. As adults, they use their feet as parachutes to glide from tree to tree.

Name: _____ Date: _____

Spiders

There is a large group of animals that do not have backbones. They are called **invertebrates**. One group, or **phylum**, of invertebrates is called **Arthropoda**. Arthropoda includes insects and spiders. Because they are similar in some respects, some people think spiders are insects, but they are not. Insects have bodies with three main parts: a head, thorax, and abdomen. The insect's head includes its mouth, eyes, and antennae. Its thorax has three pairs of legs. Spiders, on the other hand, have only two main body parts. The head and thorax are combined and called the cephalothorax. The second part is called the abdomen. The cephalothorax includes the mouth, eyes, and four pairs of legs. Spiders, along with scorpions, ticks, mites, and other animals, belong to a group called **Arachnida**. This group was named after Arachne, a girl in an ancient Greek story. In this Greek myth, Arachne made the mistake of beating Athena, who was the goddess of war and handicraft, in a weaving contest. As a punishment, Athena changed Arachne into a spider.

Spiders are important. They eat many harmful insects each day. They are also food for birds, fish, and other animals. They are important in recycling dead animals and dead trees back into the earth. They also help pollinate some plants.

1. The United States Defense Department studied spider webs in order to see if they are strong enough to be used in:
   A. Parachutes.
   B. Bulletproof vests.
   C. Electronic data transfer.
   D. Automobile tires.

2. After mating, a female black widow spider:
   A. Kills the male.
   B. Remains fertile for the rest of her life.
   C. Dies within the year.
   D. Leaves the web for food.

3. The European water spider lives:
   A. Near the water.
   B. Underwater.
   C. In the desert.
   D. In Aqua, Italy.

4. The most well-known of the black widow spiders in the United States is the southern widow. Its Latin name is *Latrodectus mactans*, which means:
   A. Assassin.
   B. Red hourglass.
   C. Black lady.
   D. Murderous, biting robber.

5. There is a spider in the Namib Desert that is a:
   A. Carpenter.   B. Tailor.   C. Stonemason.   D. Cook.

6. Among black widow spiders, the most dangerous are the:
   A. Males.   B. Females.   C. Juveniles.   D. Eggs.

62

Spiders (cont.)

7. Many young spiders travel from where they were born to another location at a distance by:
   A. Skiing.   B. Swimming.   C. Ballooning.   D. Skating.

8. Many spiders need to make a new web each day, one every day. They dispose of the old web by:
   A. Abandoning it.   B. Burying it.
   C. Rolling it up and using it as bait. D. Eating it.

9. The crab spider catches its prey by:
   A. Singing to it.   B. Sneaking up on it.
   C. Hypnotizing it.   D. Disguising itself as a flower.

10. When the male of one species of wolf spider wants to mate with a female, it:
    A. Gives her a wrapped present.   B. Dances.
    C. Sings.   D. Builds a web for her.

11. A banana spider's favorite food is:
    A. Bananas.   B. Plantains.   C. Other spiders.   D. Cockroaches.

12. Which is the most poisonous?
    A. Tarantula spider   B. Black widow spider
    C. Bee sting   D. Rattlesnake

13. In order to keep an insect it has caught away from other predators, a spider:
    A. Hides it.   B. Assigns sentries to guard it.
    C. Wraps it up.   D. Buries it.

14. The dinopidae spider is unusual. Instead of sitting in its web like many spiders, it:
    A. Decorates it with flowers. B. Throws it.
    C. Gives it to larger spiders. D. Uses it as a trampoline.

15. Hundreds of years ago, people ate mashed spiders:
    A. As a cure for a cold.   B. As a punishment.
    C. To increase their intelligence. D. To kill themselves.

16. The bola spider gets its food by:
    A. Fishing   B. Hunting   C. Stealing   D. Foraging

17. Large spider webs in New Guinea are used for:
    A. Fishing nets.   B. Hammocks.
    C. Table decorations.   D. Restraints for criminals.

18. When a tarantula gets old, it:
    A. Gets arthritis.   B. Becomes tastier.
    C. Becomes bald on its thorax. D. Moves to Florida.

Spiders—Answers

1. **B. Bulletproof vests.**
2. **B. Remains fertile for the rest of her life.** After mating, the female black widow remains fertile for the rest of her life. She is able to produce nine to twelve egg sacs, each sac containing up to 500 eggs, during her life span, which is two or three years. The story that, after mating, the female black widow always kills her mate is somewhat a myth. There are several different species of black widow spiders worldwide. Most species are not cannibalistic *in the wild.* The story that the black widow eats the male after mating began because that sometimes happens in the laboratory where the male is unable to leave after mating. The female's eyesight is not good, and she sometimes mistakes a male for an insect caught in her web if it does not get away immediately after mating. The various species of the widow spider have different appearances. The black widow spiders in the United States and Europe are shiny black and have a red "hourglass" on their undersides. Sometimes the hourglass is shaped more like an anvil or just looks like two separate spots. The female can be as much as 150 times larger than the male. The males look so different from the females that most people don't recognize them as black widow spiders. The males do have venom, but it is not as strong as that of the female. There is also a red widow spider and a brown widow spider.
3. **B. Underwater.** The only spider that lives, hunts, and mates underwater is the European water spider, even though it needs air to survive. It performs this amazing feat by trapping air above the water and bringing it underneath the surface to form an air chamber. The female will weave a silken sheet underwater, and fasten it to plants. Then she will go to the surface, capture an air bubble, take it underwater and put it beneath the silken sheet. She will do this several times until she has enough air. The sheet will arch up forming a kind of a dome. She will remain in her underwater home laying her eggs and trapping prey that wanders by.
4. **D. Murderous, biting robber.**
5. **C. Stonemason.** This spider, which lives in the Namib Desert, builds an almost perfect circle of pebbles around its burrow. It uses seven small pebbles that are all about the same size, shape, and color. Why does it do this? No one knows.
6. **B. Females.** While the male does have a poisonous bite, the male's venom sacs cease to develop and are not considered dangerous to humans. The female is not aggressive unless she is encountered while she is laying or guarding her eggs. When a person is bitten, it is very painful. There is sweating, nausea, a rise in body temperature, and a rise in blood pressure. If treated with an antitoxin, the bite is rarely fatal, except occasionally in the case of a small child.
7. **C. Ballooning.** A huge number of spiders can be born from a single egg sac at about the same time. This large number of spiders would be unable to all survive together at the same location; there would not be enough food. So it is important for most of them to leave the area and to travel as far away as possible. Different species use different methods of **dispersal**. Many species use a method that is called **ballooning**. The spider does not actually use a balloon, but uses a silk thread in order to travel through the air. This method only works for young spiders and very small spiders. When there are rising air currents and a light wind, the spider will climb to a high point and release a string of

64

Spiders—Answers (cont.)

silk. When the thread is long enough, the spider lets go of the point and begins sailing. Of course, it has no control of where it will land, and it may descend in a place that is dangerous.

8. **D. Eating it.**

9. **D. Disguising itself as a flower.** The crab spider is able to change its color to match its surroundings, which usually consists of flowers. It doesn't matter what color flower upon which a crab spider is sitting, it can change its color to match it. It will sit on a flower and blend by changing color. It will wait until a butterfly or bee approaches the flower, and then the spider will strike. It will grab its prey, inject it with poison, and then suck the juices from its body. The crab spider got its name because it is shaped like a crab and moves sideways like one.

10. **A. Gives her a wrapped present.** The present is a wrapped fly. While she is eating her present, the male will mate with her. It uses this trick so she will not eat him.

11. **D. Cockroaches.** Cockroaches live on bananas.

12. **B. Black widow spider.** A black widow's bite is 15 times more poisonous than that of a rattlesnake. In fact, black widow venom is the most poisonous material known. Of course, the amount of venom from the bite of a black widow spider is much less than that of a rattlesnake, so the bite of the black widow usually does not cause death.

13. **C. Wraps it up.** It usually wraps it in a silk ball to keep it away from other predators.

14. **B. Throws it.** It uses a handheld web. Rather than making a web, sitting on it, and waiting for an insect to fly into it, it holds the web with its front legs. When an insect comes close by, it drops the web over it, just like using a net.

15. **A. As a cure for a cold.** Oddly enough, "Little Miss Muffet" of the nursery rhyme was a real person. Her father was an expert on spiders and would force his daughter to eat mashed spiders in order to cure her colds. This was a common practice until about 200 years ago.

16. **A. Fishing.** Spiders use the silk they produce in many ways. One of the more unusual ways is a favorite with the bola spider. It does not spin a web as many spiders do but instead produces one thread that it uses as a fishing line. Instead of trying to catch fish, it fishes for moths; instead of putting the fishing line in the water, it dangles it in the air. After producing the silk thread, it puts a sticky ball at the end of it. The sticky ball has a scent that is similar to that produced by a female moth. Then the bola spider will hang upside-down, and holding onto the silk, it will swing its bait around. A male moth will catch the scent, and thinking it is a female, it will grab the sticky ball.

17. **A. Fishing nets.** South Sea Islanders use the silk to make fishing nets and bags.

18. **C. Becomes bald on its thorax.**

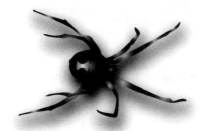

Name: _____ Date: _____

Insects: General

There are many more kinds of insects on Earth than any other kind of living creature. Insects outnumber all other animals at a rate of 4 to 1. Over one million species have been discovered and recorded, and scientists believe that there might be ten times that number that haven't been named. There are over 90,000 documented species of insects in North America alone.

While insects are pests to humans and animals and carry diseases and sometimes destroy crops, they also provide many benefits. They pollinate plants and flowers, produce honey, wax, and silk, break down and recycle plants and animals and are food for many other creatures.

People sometimes call insects "bugs." A bug is a specific type of insect called a **heteroptera**. While all bugs are insects, not all insects are bugs. Some more common bugs include stinkbugs, bedbugs, and water striders.

Insects come in all sizes, shapes, and habits, but **all** have the following four characteristics:

* three body parts—a head, thorax, and abdomen   • six jointed legs
* an exoskeleton (a skeleton on the outside)   • two antennae

If a creature does not have all four of these things, then the animal is not an insect.

1. The oarsman is an insect that catches its prey by:
   A. Hitting it with a paddle.   B. Becoming a boat.
   C. Drowning it.   D. Pretending to be its mate.

2. Adactylidium mites are born by:
   A. Crawling from the mother's mouth.   B. Eating their mother from the inside.
   C. Beehives.   D. Stagnant water.

3. Which insect kills the most humans?
   A. Tsetse fly   B. Cockroaches
   C. Mosquitoes   D. Killer bees

4. Which is *not* another name for a dragonfly?
   A. Devil's darning needle   B. Snake doctor
   C. Horse stinger   D. Mosquito hawk

5. Where is the only place on Earth where insects do *not* live?
   A. Arctic   B. Antarctica
   C. Deserts   D. Open ocean

6. You are less likely to be a target for mosquitoes if you:
   A. Are blonde.   B. Have just eaten bananas.
   C. Are a child.   D. Are an adult.

66

Name: _____ Date: _____

 Insects: General (cont.)

7. The color of insect blood is either colorless, green, or:
    A. Red　　　　B. Blue　　　　C. Yellow　　　　D. Purple

8. About how many legs does a centipede have?
    A. 2　　　　B. 40　　　　C. 100　　　　D. 1,000

9. The male praying mantis mates:
    A. After it eats flower nectar.　　　B. When it is two years old.
    C. In the spring.　　　D. When its head is torn off.

10. The offspring of one aphid in one season, if none died, would be:
    A. 1,560,000,000,000,000,000,000,000.　B. 1,560,000,000,000,000,000.
    C. 1,560,000,000.　　　D. 1,560,000.

11. The word "cooties" is really:
    A. A word made up by children.　　　B. Body lice.
    C. Ear worms.　　　D. Head beetles.

12. Female aphids are born:
    A. Only in July.　　　B. One month before males.
    C. In even numbers.　　　D. Pregnant.

13. What was the biggest insect that has ever lived?
    A. Mosquito　　　B. Dragonfly
    C. Beetle　　　D. Locust

14. People have sometimes mistaken dragonflies for:
    A. Dead ancestors　　　B. Fairies.
    C. Ball lightning.　　　D. Evil spirits.

15. By listening to the chirps of a cricket, one is able to:
    A. Tell where it comes from.　　　B. Predict an approaching hurricane.
    C. Estimate the temperature.　　　D. Tell its age.

16. The only mosquitoes that bite are:
    A. Males.　　　B. Females.
    C. Vampire mosquitoes.　　　D. North American mosquitoes.

17. Mosquitoes are attracted to the color:
    A. Red.　　　B. Blue.　　　C. White.　　　D. Flesh.

18. What is the main food of mosquitoes?
    A. Human blood　　　B. Animal blood
    C. Nectar from flowers　　　D. Aphids

Insects: General—Answers

1. **B. Becoming a boat.** The oarsman is sometimes called a backswimmer, boat fly, boatman, water boatman, and boat insect. It gets its name because it swims upside-down and its body is shaped something like a boat, with the top part of its body shaped like a keel. The oarsman is a predator that waits upside down in the water to attack tadpoles and insects. It responds quickly to the smallest vibration, and using its third pair of legs, it rows as fast as it can to the cause of the disturbance. Once it finds its prey, it pierces the skin of its prey with its beak, injects digestive enzymes, and then sucks the victim dry.

2. **B. Eating their mother from the inside.** An adactylidium's young is reared within a mother's body. They are fed, they grow, and they even mate inside the mother. When it is time for them to be born, they devour her from inside. The offspring will cut holes through their mother's body and finally emerge. The females will continue the process and live, while the single male, who has already fulfilled his reproductive role, will be born dead or dying.

3. **C. Mosquitoes.** The tsetse fly kills 66,000 people each year. While flies do carry many diseases, the most dangerous insects are mosquitoes, which pass a parasite that causes malaria and other diseases. Malaria kills one million people per year. In fact, mosquitoes are not only the most dangerous insects on Earth, they kill more people than any other animal.

4. **A, B, C, D. All answers are correct.**

5. **D. Open ocean.** Insects are adaptable creatures and have evolved to live successfully in most environments on Earth, including deserts, forests, in water, in caves, and even in frozen areas such as Antarctic. The only place where insects are not commonly found is in the oceans.

6. **D. Are an adult.** So if you are a blonde child who has just eaten bananas, you had better stay indoors.

7. **C. Yellow.** The blood of mammals is red, the blood of lobsters is blue, and the blood of insects is light green, colorless, or yellow.

8. **B. 40.** Most people think that a centipede has a hundred legs, but it doesn't. It is easy to understand how someone could make that mistake. *Ped* means foot. The prefix *cent* means 1/100th. There are 100 *cents* in a dollar. A *cent*ury has 100 years in it. So, it would

seem that *cent*ipede would be an insect that had 100 legs. While it may appear that a centipede has 100 legs, it only has about 40. The world's longest centipede is the giant scolopender of South America and Asia, which is often 11 inches long. People make the same mistake with the millipede. It seems logical that a *milli*pede would have a thousand legs. *Milli* means 1/1000. A *mill*ennium has 1,000 years. However, a millipede only has about 100 to 200 legs. The centipede is able to move faster than the

millepede when traveling, but the millepede will keep more legs on the ground than in the air. The largest millipede in the world is *Graphidostreptus gigas* of Africa, which reaches a length of 11 inches and a diameter of three-fourths of an inch.

Insects: General—Answers (cont.)

9. **D. When its head is torn off.** The female praying mantis bites off the male's head while they are mating. The male sometimes continues mating even after its head and part of its upper torso have been bitten off.

10. **A. 1,560,000,000,000,000,000,000,000.** When the weather is warm and if the host plant is healthy, an aphid can produce fifty babies in one week, which mature one week later. This makes it possible in one season for a single cabbage aphid to produce 1,560,000,000,000,000,000,000,000 offspring, if none died. By the way, if you want to read that number aloud, you say: 1 heptillion, 560 hexillion.

11. **B. Body lice.** Many people are surprised to learn that there really are such things as cooties. They may believe that the word "cooties" was just a word made up by children to describe unpleasant bugs or germs. Cooties are in fact a kind of body lice. The word is from the Malay *kutu*, which means "louse."

12. **D. Pregnant.** Before these mites are born, the unborn male fertilizes the unborn females. The females are then born already pregnant and the male dies before it is born.

13. **B. Dragonfly.** Dragonflies are ancient insects that existed before the dinosaurs. These ancient dragonflies were much larger than those that live today. The fossil of a dragonfly, Meganeura, that lived in prehistoric times, was likely the largest insect to have ever lived. It had a wingspan of over two feet. Today, the largest dragonfly is found in South America and has a wingspan of slightly over seven inches. Oddly enough, other than being smaller, the dragonflies of today do not look very different from their ancestors.

14. **B. Fairies.** This mistake has occurred for centuries. Children have told parents that they have seen fairies. Even adults have made the same claim. When these claims have been checked out, though, the fairies turned out to be dragonflies. In a way, these mistakes are understandable. The long, colorful wings and the rapid flight of dragonflies are similar to how people imagine fairies to be.

15. **C. Estimate the temperature.** Scientists have discovered that by counting how many times a cricket chirps in 15 seconds and then adding 40 to that number, one can tell about what the temperature is on the Fahrenheit scale.

16. **B. Females.** The female mosquito's mouth is designed to pierce the skin and suck blood. She is able to find her victim by following the stream of carbon dioxide the animal exhales. She lands on her victim, stabs, and sucks the blood up through a nasal tube. Her mouth works like a syringe. As she sucks the blood, she also pumps anticoagulants into the opening so the blood does not clot. Her body will enlarge and sometimes  become red because of so much blood in her abdomen. Mosquitoes prefer children over adults. At one feeding, a mosquito is able to drink one and a half times its own weight in blood. On the other hand, male mosquitoes feed only on plant juices, because their mouth parts are too weak to pierce animal skin.

17. **B. Blue.** They are attracted to this color twice as much as they are to other colors.

18. **C. Nectar from flowers.** Females only feed on blood in order to give them the protein they need to lay their eggs.

Name: _____ Date: _____

Insects: Butterflies

Like all insects, butterflies and moths have a head, thorax, abdomen, six legs, and two antennae. Unlike some other insects, butterflies and moths have four wings that are usually covered by colored scales. They also have a coiled **proboscis**. A proboscis can mean many things. When referring to a human, the proboscis is the nose. An elephant's trunk is its proboscis. But for a butterfly or moth, the proboscis is a thin, tubular, protruding mouth part used for drinking flower nectar. Butterflies and moths, which make up the second largest order of insects, belong to a group of insects called Lepidoptera. The name lepidoptera is based on two latin words. *Lepido* means "scale" and *ptera* means "wing." About 95 percent of all the *lepidoptera* are moths. What is the difference between a butterfly and a moth? There are some physical differences and differences in the lifestyles of the two, but the most obvious difference is that most moths tend to fly mainly at night, while butterflies are active during the day.

1. The Morgan's sphinx hawk moth from Madagascar has a proboscis (tube mouth) that is:
   A.   3 inches long.   B.   9 inches long.
   C.   6 inches long.   D.   12 inches long.

2. When many butterflies gather around standing water to drink, it is called a:
   A.   Grand gathering.   B.   Puddle party.
   C.   Host.   D.   Alliance.

3. Which of the following has the most muscles?
   A.   Caterpillar   B.   Human
   C.   Grasshopper   D.   Elephant

4. When bats approach, an Arctiid moth:
   A.   Dies of fright.   B.   Falls to the ground.
   C.   Sounds an alarm.   D.   Pretends to be a butterfly.

5. A male Indian moon moth can detect a female's scent from up to:
   A. $\frac{1}{2}$ mile away.   B.   1 mile away.
   C.   3 miles away.   D.   5 miles away.

6. A butterfly tastes with its:
   A.   Mouth.   B.   Nose.
   C.   Feet   D.   Antennae.

7. The Mexican jumping bean:
   A.   Is really a pea.   B.   Jumps because a caterpillar is inside.
   C.   Jumps so it doesn't get eaten.   D.   Doesn't really exist.

8. Butterflies live longer:
   A.   Without heads.   B.   If they do not mate.
   C.   If they are given bottled water.   D.   When the temperature is above 90°.

70

Insects: Butterflies (cont.)

9. If attacked, an Eastern tent caterpillar moth will defend itself by:
   A. Attacking the approaching predator.
   B. Having a spider protect it.
   C. Emitting a loud scream.
   D. Poisoning its attacker.

10. The young of the polyphemous moth, which feed on broad-leaved trees, increase their body weight _____ in two months.
    A. 1,000 times
    B. 20,000 times
    C. 40,000 times
    D. 80,000 times

11. How many different kinds of moths and butterflies are there in the world?
    A. 252
    B. 218,500
    C. 75,500
    D. 576,500

12. The ghost moth can whistle through its:
    A. Mouth.
    B. Tongue.
    C. Nose.
    D. Ears.

13. In order to avoid bats, some moths:
    A. Have ears on their wings.
    B. Use echolocation (sonar).
    C. Travel in pairs.
    D. Fly close to the ground.

14. Butterflies have:
    A. Stingers.
    B. Biting jaws.
    C. Green blood.
    D. The ability to adjust their temperature.

15. In the winter, monarch butterflies in North America:
    A. Migrate.
    B. Die.
    C. Enclose themselves in a cocoon.
    D. Hibernate in Texas.

16. The butterfly uses its _____ for smelling and its feet for tasting.
    A. Nose
    B. Antennae
    C. Mouth
    D. Feet

17. The butterfly breathes through its _____ because it doesn't have lungs.
    A. Nose
    B. Eyes
    C. Body
    D. Feet

Insects: Butterflies—Answers

1. **D. 12 inches long.** There is an orchid in Madagascar, an island nation in the Indian Ocean, just off the eastern coast of Africa, that survives with the help of the sphinx hawk moth. The nectar in this orchid is produced deep within a thin tube in the flower. The nectar is so difficult to reach that bees and butterflies are unable to reach it, so they are unable to carry its pollen from one flower to the other. That is where the Madagascan Morgan's sphinx hawk moth comes in. With what might be the longest tongue in the insect world, this moth is able to feed on this hard-to-get nectar, and in the process, it carries the pollen from flower to flower.

2. **B. Puddle party.** Butterflies need a water supply. They will gather in groups at a puddle and drink the standing water in order to get the moisture and minerals they need.

3. **D. Elephant.** Humans have 639 muscles, while an adult grasshopper has about 900 muscles. A butterfly caterpillar has about 4,000 muscles with about 248 of those muscles in its head. The elephant has 100,000 muscles in its trunk alone.

4. **C. Sounds an alarm.** Different animals use various methods to avoid a predator. Some use bright colors as a signal to the predator that they are poisonous or do not taste good. The Arctiid moth uses a different method. When a bat approaches, the moth emits a series of clicks that warns the bat that it does not taste good. Tiger moths also emit clicks when a bat approaches. Scientists believe that this clicking sound confuses the approaching bat that thinks it has located its prey by using echolocation. Echolocation is a process bats use to fly in the dark. The bat makes a high-pitched sound that echoes off objects. This tells the bat how far away objects are by how quickly the sound comes back to it. The clicking of the moth interferes with this process.

5. **C. 3 miles away.** A male Indian moon moth has a sense of smell that is one of the best in all of nature. In addition to being able to detect a female that is three miles away, the male has another method of making sure that the female's scent is not picked up by other males. It is able to release its own substance, which blocks other males from picking up the scent of a female it is following.

6. **C. Feet.** When a butterfly lands on a plant, it immediately determines if this is the kind of plant it prefers.

7. **B. Jumps because a caterpillar is inside.** The Mexican jumping bean is amusing to watch. In warm weather, these seed capsules roll, jerk, and skip along the ground, However, they don't really jump, and they aren't really beans. These seed capsules are able to keep this motion up for several months because inside is a grub or larva of a small, gray moth named, appropriately enough, the jumping bean moth (*Laspeyresia saltitans*). How did the grub get inside the seed capsule? The jumping bean moth lays its eggs on the plant's female flowers, and the developing caterpillars eat the seed as it develops. The seed capsules fall to the ground, and the caterpillar makes a cocoon inside the seed. After eating the seed within the capsule section, the strong larva throws itself from one wall to the other, causing the jumping movements of the seed capsule.

8. **A. Without heads.** If a caterpillar's head is removed carefully, the caterpillar will develop normally and become a chrysalis. A chrysalis is a pupa, especially of a moth or butterfly, enclosed in a cocoon. When the butterfly emerges from the cocoon, it will be a healthy

Butterflies—Answers (cont.)

butterfly without a head. Headless butterflies often live longer than those with a head. Scientists believe that they live longer because they do not have as much stress.

9. **D. Poisoning its attacker.** The Eastern tent caterpillar moth lays its eggs and then builds a large tent to cover them. When the caterpillars hatch, they remain in the tent and eat the leaves and the empty egg cases. As the food in the tent becomes scarce, the caterpillars move to the top of the tent to eat leaves. When they eat, they collect cyanide, which is a poison, from the tree. If attacked, the caterpillars vomit the cyanide, which discourages the predator.

10. **D. 80,000 times.** The caterpillar of the polyphemus moth eats 86,000 times its birth weight in a little under two months; that would be the same as a seven-pound baby eating over 300 tons of food.

11. **B. 218,500.** About 200,000 species of moths have been found and classified. Scientists believe there are many more that have not yet been discovered. Some scientists believe there may be a million or more different species of moths in the world. There are about 18,500 species of butterflies that have been identified. There are approximately 750 species of butterflies in the United States.

12. **B. Tongue.**

13. **A. Have ears on their wings.** Many species of moths have a tiny structure near the root of each wing that can best be described as an ear. It is a membrane-covered cavity that is linked to sensory nerves and wired into the moth's nervous system. While the moth uses this "ear" to communicate with other moths, scientists are convinced that this was originally developed to detect the high-frequency sounds of a bat.

14. **C. Green blood.** Butterflies do not have hemoglobin, which makes the blood of humans and many other animals red. Most insect blood is either colorless or a light green. Without biting jaws or stingers that other insects have, butterflies must rely on their coloration or speed to survive. Butterflies are cold-blooded and cannot regulate their body temperature. They need to warm their wings in the sun before they can fly.

15. **A. Migrate.** Most species of butterflies spend their winter in a chrysalis form, while other species hibernate under bark and leaves. Monarch butterflies in North America deal with winter in an unusual way for butterflies. Monarchs cannot survive the cold winter temperatures of the northern states, so they migrate and hibernate in warmer areas. Monarchs that live east of the Rockies migrate 2,500 miles to Mexico while monarchs that live west of the Rockies migrate to southern California. When they first arrive at their winter destinations, monarchs gather into clusters in trees. These clusters become larger and more compact as the weather becomes colder. In spring when warm weather approaches, the clusters begin to break up, and the butterflies search for food. When the weather warms up even more, the monarchs will reproduce and their offspring will make the flight back north. The monarchs will mate up to seven times during the summer. Each butterfly will live from two to six weeks. When autumn approaches, non-reproductive monarchs are born, and they migrate south.

16. **B. Antennae.**

17. **C. Body.**

Name: _____ Date: _____

 ## Hidden Insects

Directions: The names of several insects are hidden in the unusual sentences shown below. Find the insects by looking within words or between two or more words and underline them; ignore punctuation marks. The first insect is underlined as an example.

1. I have always <u>bee</u>n a happy person.
2. "I can't find the buggy," the mother complained.
3. I owe evil men a lot of money.
4. The mammoth was a prehistoric creature.
5. She stopped here briefly on her way to the store.
6. The swimmer was caught in the Cayman tide.
7. At the end of the term, itemize what you have learned.
8. The class was prepared for the tornado drill.
9. The holy man held the chalice for all to see.
10. The girl in the pink blouse played a beautiful tune on her bugle.
11. He was the best of leaders.
12. Beware of the booby trap hidden on the trail.
13. Their soccer team was the best among nations.
14. Warranties can always be extended.
15. "You may approach the bench," the judge said.

What's the Difference?

Directions: Explain the differences between each of the animals in the following pairs.

1. Turtle—Tortoise _____

_____

_____

2. Alligator—Crocodile _____

_____

_____

_____

3. Butterfly—Moth _____

_____

_____

_____

Name: _____ Date: _____

Insects: Bees and Wasps

The insects that are the most beneficial to humans can be found in the insect order **Hymenoptera**. Some of the members of this order include bees and wasps. Bees and others in this order pollinate fruits, vegetables, and flowers. Wasps are parasites that feed on insects that are pests. Without wasps and other parasites, the pests they eat would destroy most crops. Yellowjackets, hornets, and wasps feed flies and caterpillars to their young.

1. Scientists tell us that bumblebees should not be able to:
   A. Produce honey.   B. Fly.
   C. See red.   D. Live together.

2. Honeybees collect nectar from over _____ separate flowers in order to make one pound of honey.
   A. 2,000   B. 20,000
   C. 2,000,000   D. 2,000,000,000

3. It is estimated that what percentage of all human food depends on bees?
   A. 0.3%   B. 3%
   C. 13%   D. 30%

4. When a honeybee finds fresh flowers, it flies back to the hive and tells the rest of the hive the location of the flowers by:
   A. Sign language.   B. Buzzing.
   C. Eye blinking.   D. Dancing.

5. Bees are now being trained to detect:
   A. Cancer.   B. Drugs.
   C. Terrorists.   D. Landmines.

6. When the temperature gets hot, honeybees:
   A. Air-condition their hives. B. Go swimming.
   C. Work only at night.   D. Sweat.

7. To collect a pound of honey, bees must fly this approximate distance:
   A. From Boston to London.   B. Twice around the world.
   C. From Earth to the moon.   D. From Earth to Mars.

8. On the average, how many meals is a worker larva fed each day?
   A. 3   B. 30   C. 130   D. 1,300

Name: _____ Date: _____

Insects: Bees and Wasps (cont.)

9. After a honeybee stings, it:
    A. Grows another stinger.   B. Becomes a drone.
    C. Dies.   D. Is banished from the hive.

10. The worker bees in the hive are:
    A. Male.   B. Female.
    C. Male or female.   D. Neither.

11. The only purpose of the male bee is to:
    A. Forage for nectar or pollen.   B. Mate with the queen.
    C. Build the hive.   D. Find a field of clover.

12. What kills the most people in the United States each year?
    A. Bees   B. Wasps
    C. Snakes   D. Sharks

13. Wasps build their nests out of:
    A. Spider webs.   B. Papier-mâché.
    C. Sticks.   D. Straw.

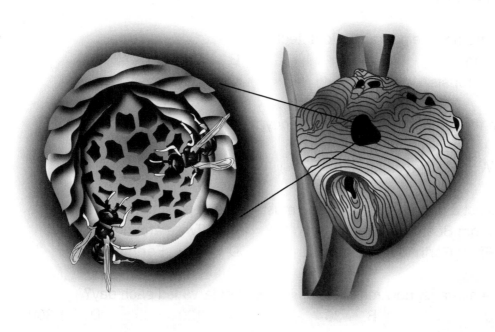

Amazing Facts in Science
Insects: Bees and Wasps

Insects: Bees and Wasps—Answers

1. **C. See red.** Some students probably answered "fly." There is a myth that a bumblebee should be unable to fly, based on its body size and wing size. It is true that, in the 1930s, a professor of aerodynamics was asked about the aerodynamics of wasps' and bees' wings at a party. He made some quick calculations, which seemed to prove that bees should not be able to fly with such small wings. He later studied the problem more carefully and learned that his calculations were made with the assumption that the bee's wings were rigid, but they are not. They bend and twist, pushing the bee's body up on both the fore and back strokes. While many people heard about the scientist's original calculation, they never heard about the second, so the myth continues to this day.

2. **C. 2,000,000.** The average worker honeybee makes about 1/12 of a teaspoon of honey in its lifetime.

3. **D. 30%.** The pollination provided by bees is important to many crops. According to scientists, the domesticated honeybee population has declined by about 50%. Some farmers, such as almond farmers in California, say their yields have dropped because of the lack of domestic bees to pollinate their crops. The decline, which has been occurring both in the domestic and the wild bee populations, is caused by disease. Many different mites and parasites have taken their toll. Widespread use of pesticides on farms is also cited as a cause.

4. **D. Dancing.** If a honeybee finds fresh flowers, she will go back to the hive and do a complicated dance, which explains to the other bees in the hive what she has found, where it is located, and how far away it is. The dance moves are based on the angle of the flowers in relationship to the position of the sun and the distance to the food. If the bee dances in a circle, it means the food is within 100 yards. Dancing in a figure-eight movement means it is farther away. The other bees in the hive understand this dance and are able to find the flowers.

5. **D. Landmines.** It is estimated that over 80 million landmines are buried in various countries around the world. Each year more than 15,000 people, many of them children, are killed by these mines. Since the mines are hidden, finding and disarming them is difficult. Many detection methods have been tried. High-tech methods have been tried with some success, but up until recently, the most successful technique was to use dogs to locate mines through smell. However, dogs must be led by humans, which makes this technique very risky. A company in Belgium now trains giant African pouch rats to find buried landmines. The University of Montana is training bees to find the mines. Both the rats and the bees are trained to detect the odors associated with explosives. Both have been highly successful. These two creatures make the detection of landmines less expensive and safer for humans.

© Mark Twain Media, Inc., Publishers
77

Insects: Bees and Wasps—Answers (cont.)

6. **A. Air-condition their hives.** The temperature inside the hive must be kept constant. During the summer months, the hive temperature rises, so the bees work to cool it. The worker bees store water in their stomachs and bring it into the hive. They then beat their wings to fan the moisture from their bodies onto the honeycomb in order to reduce the hive's temperature. In the winter, the problem is just the opposite—the bees must heat the hive. In order to do this, the bees eat more honey than they do in warmer weather to provide energy with which to warm themselves. They will huddle together to keep warm.

7. **B. Twice around the world.**

8. **D. 1,300.**

9. **C. Dies.** The bumblebee does not die when it stings; it can sting repeatedly. The honeybee, however, is the only bee that dies after it stings because its stinger has barbs that face backward. These barbs prevent the bee from removing the stinger. The stinger not only stays in the victim, but so does a part of the bee's abdomen, which continues to pump venom.

10. **B. Female.** Most of the bees in the hives are workers, and all are female and do all of the work. They build the honeycomb, clean the hive, feed the queen, collect the food, and care for the larvae. Strangely enough, their jobs change as they get older. After they are hatched, the worker bee cleans for three days. Then she becomes a nurse and feeds the queen and the larvae. When her wax glands mature and she is able to produce wax, she spends her time building honeycombs. Between days 16 to 20, she takes the pollen and nectar brought to the hive by the older bees and puts it into the comb; then, for a few days, she guards the hive. As she nears the end of her life, she collects nectar and pollen for the hive.

11. **B. Mate with the queen.** Male bees are called **drones**. Only a few males are hatched in the hive. After hatching, they are fed by the workers, then they fly off to find a queen. When a queen is found, the male mates with her in the air and then dies. Drone bees do not have a stinger.

12. **A. Bees.** Most insect sting reactions only hurt, itch, swell, and cause redness. Sometimes the sting will become infected and have more serious consequences. However, the most serious consequence of a bee sting is an allergic reaction. While some reactions are mild, the most severe can cause problems— breathing difficulty, swelling of the tongue, dizziness, or even death.

13. **B. Papier-mâché.** Unlike bees who use wax to construct their combs, wasps chew trees and fence posts in order to construct their papier-mâché nests. The nest is strong, durable, and surprisingly lightweight. A new colony is created when a queen emerges from hibernation and picks a nest site on a branch, building, or in a similar location. She then makes paper by chewing on wood and other plant fibers and mixes it with saliva. She spits out the mixture and dabs it on the nest site. When dried, this pulp forms the stem for the nest. She then adds a few hexagonal cells to the bottom of the stem and lays a single egg in each one. The new generation of wasps hatches and begins building more paper cells into which the queen will lay additional eggs.

Name: _____   Date: _____

Insects: Ants

Ants are small insects that are strong for their size and live in colonies. Each colony is made up of at least one queen, female workers, drones, eggs, larvae, and pupae. Each ant has a very special job. There are almost 20,000 species of ants in various sizes, colors, and habits. The largest ant species is over an inch in length, and the smallest is about 1/25 of an inch. Ants live almost everywhere except in extremely cold locations. Some species build mounds, others live in underground tunnels, while still others live inside trees. Ants lead busy lives. They plant gardens; herd and milk bugs, such as aphids; have armies; engage in battles; take slaves; and bury their dead in ant cemeteries.

Ants are predators of other insects and some small animals. They scavenge and eat more than 90% of the bodies of small dead animals. Many plants and animals depend on ants for their survival. If ants were to suddenly die out, hundreds of thousands of species would become extinct, and the world's ecosystems would be destroyed.

1. "White ants" is another name for:
   A. Lice.
   C. Termites.
   B. European ants.
   D. Flour ants.

2. The weaver ant builds its nest by:
   A. Sewing grass.
   C. Weaving straw.
   B. Gluing leaves.
   D. Weaver oaks.

3. All of the work in a typical ant colony is:
   A. Done by males.
   C. Shared by males and females.
   B. Done by females.
   D. Done by slaves.

4. Ants are:
   A. Harmful.
   C. Both harmful and helpful.
   B. Helpful.
   D. Neither harmful nor helpful.

5. For more than 3,000 years, carpenter ants have been used to:
   A. Close wounds.
   C. Catch fish.
   B. Build bookcases.
   D. Add protein to cakes.

6. Some ant species can survive underwater for:
   A. Four hours.
   C. Four days.
   B. Fourteen hours.
   D. Fourteen days.

7. Who were the world's first farmers?
   A. Ants
   C. Termites
   B. Humans
   D. Bark beetles

Name: _____ Date: _____

Insects: Ants (cont.)

8. A honeypot ant:
   A. Lives in a beehive.
   C. Is a living storage container.
   B. Is shaped like a honeypot.
   D. Feeds only on honey.

9. When the only queen ant dies:
   A. The colony dies.
   C. A queen is taken from another colony.
   B. A new queen is elected.
   D. The king takes over.

10. Which one of the following methods are *not* used by army ants to communicate?
    A. Chemical signals
    C. Vibrations
    B. Touch
    D. Visual signs

11. An ant species found in Malaysia, *Camponotus saundersi*, has an unusual method of defense. When there is a battle, the ant:
    A. Throws baby ants at the attacker.
    C. Explodes.
    B. Dances.
    D. Disguises itself.

12. Some primitive cultures have used ants for:
    A. Pets.
    C. Watchdogs.
    B. Candy.
    D. Jewelry.

Insects: Ants—Answers

1. **C. Termites.** White ants are not ants at all—they are termites. They are called white ants because most of them are small, white, social insects that live in colonies as ants do. They are not closely related to ants but are closely related to cockroaches.

2. **B. Gluing leaves.** Weaver ants make their nests by rolling up leaves and gluing them together with silk from the ants' own larvae. Here is how they do it. A row of adult ants will pull the edges of a leaf together. At the same time, other ants will put an ant larva in its jaw and squeeze until the larva produces a glue-like silken thread. It is almost the same as a person squeezing a tube of toothpaste. They continue this process along the edges of the leaf until the leaf edges stick together.

3. **B. Done by females.** In the colony, only the queens lay eggs. The males' only function is to mate with the queen and die. Worker ants are all females. They are responsible for finding food, repairing the nest, and defending the colony.

   One of the biggest ant colonies ever discovered was found on the Ishikari coast of Hokkaido. It is estimated that one million queens and 306 million worker ants all lived in 45,000 interconnected nests, covering an area of 1.7 square miles.

4. **C. Both harmful and helpful.** Ants can be either helpful or harmful, but, for the most part, they are helpful to humans. Their tunnels and nests allow air to get into the soil. Some ants eat small insects that are harmful to plants and crops. They eat undesirable plants and recycle decomposing matter. Some even help spread seeds. On the other hand, many species of ants become house pests. Carpenter ants tunnel into wood, although they do not eat it as termites do. The fire ant has a painful bite and is a pest to both humans and livestock.

5. **A. Close wounds.** In Asia and South America, ants have been used by surgeons and medicine men to close wounds and incisions. The ants are forced to use their powerful jaws to bite together the edges of an open wound. Then the ants' heads are cut from their bodies. The jaws of the ants will remain locked until the incision heals.

6. **D. Fourteen days.** Ants are among the most adaptable creatures on Earth. When moved to a different climate, they adapt very quickly. Some ant species are capable of surviving underwater for fourteen days or longer, by going into something similar to suspended animation.

7. **A. Ants.** Humans are the fourth animal to discover farming, after ants, termites, and bark beetles. Ants of the so-called "attine" group were the first animals to deliberately grow their own food. They began farming sometime after dinosaurs became extinct. They grew fungi inside their nests and harvested it for meals. Termites and bark beetles also grow fungi and had done so many years before humans began farming.

   However, growing crops is not the only farming that ants do. Some species of ants use aphids as "cows." They stroke the aphids, and the aphids give the ants a sweet liquid called honeydew, which the ants drink. In return, the ants take care of the aphids. They take the aphids to their food plants and shelter the aphid eggs in their nests during the winter. Ants build shelters for the aphids, defend them from predators, and even take them into their nests during bad weather.

Insects: Ants—Answers (cont.)

8. **C. Is a living storage container.** A certain type of honeypot ant becomes a living storage container. Its bloated abdomen contains a liquid food that is fed to other members of the colony. Ants are different from honeybees; they do not create wax combs in which to store liquid foods. Some species produce individual ants that serve as living food containers called honeypots. At times, when the colony has abundant honeydew and nectar from plants, aphids, or other insects, worker ants feed young adult workers these liquids. Over a period of time, the honeypot ants become so full they cannot walk. They hang from the roofs of storerooms until food becomes scarce. When this occurs, the honeypot ants regurgitate the liquids they have stored, so others in the colony can eat. When a honeypot ant is stretched to its maximum size, it is about the size of a blueberry. It may fall from the ceiling and burst open, killing itself. Native Americans in the southwest have been known to eat honeypot ants as candy or medicine.

9. **A. The colony dies.** Without a queen, no new workers are born.

10. **D. Visual signs.** All ants, including army ants, can communicate in many ways. Their most important method of communication is with chemical signals. Chemicals, which scientists call pheromones, are released into the air and signal an alarm, which could be a need for food, assistance, or other information. Chemicals are also used by workers to mark trails. They do this by wiping their abdomens on the ground as they walk. In addition to chemical communication, army ants use touch and vibrations to communicate. Since army ants are almost blind, they cannot communicate visually.

    Army ants are gluttonous predators. They hold tightly to one another and march. There may be as many as 500,000 ants in a group, looking for food and attacking any animals in their path. They are so vicious, they often kill lizards, birds, snakes, pigs, and even animals as large as horses. Larger animals are usually able to escape from the marching colony unless the animals are sleeping, hurt, or in a pen. In these cases, they may be killed and eaten.

11. **C. Explodes.** The *Camponotus saundersi* ant colony has three groups, one of which is composed of soldier ants. The soldiers must defend the colony no matter what. During a battle, they become stressed and contract their abdominal muscles, which causes them to explode and spray poison on their attackers.

12. **B. Candy.** Up until the twentieth century, Native American tribes and Mexicans would excavate honeypot ant colonies in order to snack on the ants that were swelled up with "honey." They would hold the head and thorax with their fingers, bite off the abdomen, and suck the contents into their mouths. The ants' bodies were bitter, so they weren't eaten. People who have tried this say that the "honey" tastes like molasses.

Name: _____ Date: _____

Ants Are Everywhere

Directions: Read each definition below. Then fill in the missing letters of the word the definition describes.

1. A continent <u>A</u> <u>N</u> <u>T</u> __ __ __ __ __ __

2. Found on the heads of insects <u>A</u> <u>N</u> <u>T</u> __ __ __ __ __

3. A gazelle is an example of this horned mammal <u>A</u> <u>N</u> <u>T</u> __ __ __ __ __ __

4. A work of art or furniture made in an earlier period <u>A</u> <u>N</u> <u>T</u> __ __ __ __

5. Bone-like growths on the head of a deer <u>A</u> <u>N</u> <u>T</u> __ __ __ __

6. Another word for plentiful __ __ __ __ __ <u>A</u> <u>N</u> <u>T</u>

7. Huge; enormous __ __ __ <u>A</u> <u>N</u> <u>T</u> __ __

8. An attitude of superiority to others __ __ __ __ __ <u>A</u> <u>N</u> <u>T</u>

9. A helper __ __ __ __ __ __ <u>A</u> <u>N</u> <u>T</u>

10. A substance, such as oil, used to reduce friction __ __ __ __ __ __ __ <u>A</u> <u>N</u> <u>T</u>

11. To put a seed in the ground __ __ <u>A</u> <u>N</u> <u>T</u>

12. The largest living land animal __ __ __ __ __ <u>A</u> <u>N</u> <u>T</u>

13. The young stage of a human __ __ __ <u>A</u> <u>N</u> <u>T</u>

14. The name of an ocean __ __ __ <u>A</u> <u>N</u> <u>T</u> __ __

15. Extremely intelligent __ __ __ __ __ __ <u>A</u> <u>N</u> <u>T</u>

16. To desire something __ <u>A</u> <u>N</u> <u>T</u>

17. To sing or recite in a repetitive monotonous tone __ __ <u>A</u> <u>N</u> <u>T</u>

18. A newcomer to a country __ __ __ __ __ __ <u>A</u> <u>N</u> <u>T</u>

19. Another name for trousers __ <u>A</u> <u>N</u> <u>T</u> __

20. Extremely happy __ __ __ __ __ <u>A</u> <u>N</u> <u>T</u>

Name: _____ Date: _____

Insects: Beetles

Ninety-five percent of all of the animals on Earth are insects. Scientists have discovered over one million species of insects and some believe there are as many as ten times that number that haven't yet been named.

In order to be classified as an insect, an animal must have:

- Three body parts: a head, thorax, and an abdomen;
- An exoskeleton (outside skeleton);
- Six jointed legs; and
- Two antennae.

There are 32 groups (orders) of insects. The largest is **Coleoptera**, which includes beetles. It is estimated that one out of every four animals in the world is a beetle.

1. How does a group of blister larvae work together in order to eat pollen and nectar provided by bees? The larvae:
   - A. Form the shape of a female bee.
   - B. Pretend to be baby bees.
   - C. Disguise themselves as flowers.
   - D. Attack the hive.

2. The heaviest known insect is the Goliath beetle of equatorial Africa. One was found that weighed:
   - A. One and a half ounces.
   - B. Two and a half ounces.
   - C. Three and a half ounces.
   - D. Four and a half ounces.

3. Beetles are the biggest group of insects. How many species have been identified so far?
   - A. 35
   - B. 3,500
   - C. 35,000
   - D. 350,000

4. A statue of a woman holding this insect stands in Enterprise, Alabama.
   - A. Mosquito
   - B. Cockroach
   - C. Boll weevil
   - D. Junebug

5. For which of the following does the dung beetle *not* use dung?
   - A. Food
   - B. A nursery
   - C. A wedding feast
   - D. A home

6. The jewel beetle larvae has one of the longest _____ in the insect world.
   - A. Antennae
   - B. Life spans
   - C. Legs
   - D. Stingers

7. Which is the speediest?
   - A. A male Olympic sprinter
   - B. A tiger beetle
   - C. A tropical cockroach
   - D. An ant

Name: _____ Date: _____

Insects: Beetles (cont.)

8. The short-circuit beetle is a type of bostrichid beetle that:
   - A. Breeds in electrical circuit boxes.
   - B. Chews through lead-shielded cables.
   - C. Nests in electrical outlets.
   - D. Glows in the dark.

9. What makes the rhinoceros beetle different from other beetles?
   - A. It is the prettiest.
   - B. It lives longer.
   - C. It is the strongest.
   - D. It has no mouth.

10. The female of one firefly species imitates the light pattern of the male of another species:
    - A. To mate with it.
    - B. To warn it of danger.
    - C. To eat it.
    - D. To use its light to look for food.

11. In Asia, people raise diving beetles for:
    - A. Jewelry.
    - B. Food.
    - C. Fishing.
    - D. Pets.

12. An important function carrion beetles perform is to:
    - A. Bury dead animals.
    - B. Pollinate flowers.
    - C. Eat aphids.
    - D. Kill scorpions.

13. The carrion beetle is able to smell a dead mouse:
    - A. One mile away.
    - B. Two miles away.
    - C. Five miles away.
    - D. Ten miles away.

14. The carrion beetle is not a favorite food of other animals because:
    - A. It has a spiny shell.
    - B. It contains a poison.
    - C. It smells and tastes like rotting flesh.
    - D. It looks like a cactus.

15. The ancient Egyptians thought a giant scarab beetle:
    - A. Lived underground.
    - B. Created the earth.
    - C. Had the power to heal.
    - D. Pushed the sun across the sky.

16. Which of the following is *not* the common name of a beetle?
    - A. Museum beetle
    - B. Diving beetle
    - C. Kissing beetle
    - D. Carpet beetle

17. Australians imported 45 species of:
    - A. Honeybees.
    - B. Fireflies.
    - C. Dung beetles.
    - D. Lady beetles.

Insects: Beetles—Answers

1. **A. Form the shape of a female bee.** Newborn blister beetle larvae imitate a female bee in order to get back to the bee's nest. They don't individually imitate a female bee, but as a group will gather themselves into a female bee's shape. They also give off an odor that smells like a female bee. When the male bee is attracted to the impostor, the beetle larvae attach themselves to the bee; then, when the male bee finds a real female, the beetle larvae will then transfer to her. She will unknowingly take them back to her nest, which has pollen and nectar intended for the bee eggs. Once inside the nest, the blister beetle larvae become parasites and live off the nectar, pollen, and bee eggs.

2. **C. Three and a half ounces.** It was five inches long.

3. **D. 350,000.**

4. **C. Boll weevil.** The citizens of Enterprise, Alabama, claim that this statue of a woman in a gown holding a boll weevil above her head is the only monument in the world honoring a pest. Why is there a monument to a pest that has caused and still causes millions of dollars worth of damage annually? The story begins in the latter part of the nineteenth century. The boll weevil entered from Mexico and gradually worked its way up to Enterprise, Alabama. The infestation of the weevils was so devastating that it not only caused countless cotton farmers to go broke and lose their farms, but it destroyed the local economy. A local businessman decided to fight back. He convinced a local farmer to diversify his crops by planting peanuts. He even provided money for the experiment. The experiment was successful, and other farmers followed his example. The monument is a tribute to the boll weevil for forcing farmers to diversify crops.

5. **D. A home.** Dung beetles get rid of much of the dung left by other creatures. They eat much of the droppings, and they form the remaining droppings into balls the size of tennis balls and bury them. After they breed, they use one of the balls as a wedding feast. They then make several other balls, bury each one, lay one egg, and then cover it all up. The ball acts as a nursery as well as a food pantry. The egg will hatch and feed on the balls of dung, and the grub will eventually turn into an adult and emerge. If it weren't for the dung beetle, the world would be a smellier and more unpleasant place in which to live.

6. **B. Life spans.** The life spans of some species of the adult jewel beetle is quite short. They may live for a couple of days or for a couple of weeks. While the life span of the adult jewel beetles is short (depending on the species), the larvae of the jewel beetle has one of the longest life spans in the insect world. They eat wood and lay their eggs under the bark of a live tree. The larvae are mainly wood-borers that tunnel into the trunks and branches of trees. The larvae continue to live, even if the tree is cut down and made into furniture. They may exist in the furniture for as long as forty years before the adult finally emerges.

7. **B. A tiger beetle.** Certainly if one would put these four competitors in the same race, the human would win. But if you consider each one's size, the human would not have a chance. Tropical cockroaches have been recorded running at 3.5 miles per hour, or 50 body lengths per second. This would be like a human running as fast as a racing car. Many believe it is the fastest animal for its size. However, researchers have determined that the Australian tiger beetle is even faster. One tiger beetle has been timed at 5.6 miles per hour. That would be like a man running at 730 miles per hour.

Insects: Beetles—Answers (cont.)

8. **B. Chews through lead-shielded cables.** This lets moisture into the cable and causes a short circuit.

9. **C. It is the strongest.** It only weighs two ounces but is able to carry something 850 times its weight. That would be like a 200-pound man carrying something that weighed 170,000 pounds!

10. **C. To eat it.** Fireflies flash at each other to attract mates. The male will flash a certain light pattern, and the female waiting close by will answer by repeating the same light pattern, so the male can find her. Each species of firefly has its own light pattern, so different species do not attract or respond to another firefly species. There is one species, however, where the female purposely imitates the light pattern of another species. When the male that flashed the pattern flies over to her to mate, the female that faked the pattern eats him.

11. **B. Food.**

12. **A. Bury dead animals.** Whenever a carrion beetle smells a dead animal, it rushes to bury it. After burying it, it removes the dead animal's fur or feathers and makes the flesh into a ball upon which it feeds. The female carrion beetle will lay her eggs in the ball of rotting flesh so when the grubs are hatched, they have plenty food.

13. **B. Two miles away.**

14. **C. It smells and tastes like rotting flesh.**

15. **D. Pushed the sun across the sky.** Many ancient people were fascinated with beetles, but the Egyptians made the scarab an important, sacred part of their religion. This scarab, found in jewelry and many paintings, was actually a dung beetle. The dung beetle makes the dung into a ball, rolls it along the ground, and places it underground; eventually, a new beetle emerges. The Egyptians believed that the giant scarab was a god of the sun who rolled the sun across the sky and buried it each evening. A new sun emerged each day, and Khepri, the sacred scarab, rolled the sun across the sky again.

16. **C. Kissing beetle.** Museum beetles often live in museums because they eat animals that have been stuffed and preserved. Diving beetles spend much of their time underwater. They are able to move quickly through the water, using their legs like oars. The diving beetle is able to stay underwater for a long time by sticking its breathing tube above the surface. It feeds on other insects, small fish, and snails. Carpet beetles live in homes. They lay their eggs in carpets. The grub of the carpet beetle, called a woolly bear, chews holes in carpets.

17. **C. Dung beetles.** Since cattle are not native to Australia, the dung beetles in Australia had not evolved to dispose of cattle dung. The native dung beetles' job was to get rid of the dung of kangaroos and other animals living there. So when farmers brought cattle to Australia, there was a problem—cattle produce a lot of waste. Each animal drops about 12 pads a day, which can total up to seven tons a year. With no dung beetles to dispose of the waste, the fertile grazing land was being spoiled. The good grass was replaced by coarse, foul grass that the cattle would not eat. In addition, with all of the cattle waste, flies thrived. The Australians met this challenge by importing 45 different species of dung beetles from other countries. While not all of the species survived, those that did are cleaning up the environment.

Name: _____ Date: _____

 # Insects: Cockroaches

There are more than 3,500 species of cockroaches. Cockroaches prefer dark, warm, humid environments and are often found in the tropics. But they are able to live in almost any environment and have been on Earth longer than any other winged insect.

Cockroaches are scavengers that usually feed at night. Their diet consists of many things, including food, paper, clothing, dead animals, and plants. The flattened bodies of cockroaches make it possible for them to crawl into small spaces.

1. If you cut off a cockroach's head, it will:
   A. Bleed to death.   B. Die of shock.
   C. Starve to death.   D. Die of thirst.

2. Most species of cockroaches live in:
   A. Bathrooms.   B. Kitchens.
   C. Basements.   D. The woods.

3. To scare away predators, there is a cockroach in Madagascar that:
   A. Barks.   B. Hisses.
   C. Growls.   D. Puffs up.

4. In Nova Scotia, cockroaches are called:
   A. Yankee settlers.   B. Dirty strangers.
   C. Kitchen helpers.   D. Dungy guests.

5. Cockroaches belong to a suborder of insects called *Blattaria*, which means:
   A. Dirty bugs.   B. Winged insects.
   C. To shun the light.   D. Sleeps all day.

6. The word cockroach comes from the Spanish word "cucaracha," which means:
   A. Crazy bug.   B. Salsa-eater.
   C. Dancing bug.   D. Hard to kill.

7. Another name for the brown-banded cockroach is the:
   A. Dizzy cockroach.   B. TV cockroach
   C. American idol.   D. Army cockroach.

8. The world's largest roach lives in South America and has a _____ wingspan.
   A. Six-inch   B. One-foot
   C. Two-foot   D. Three-foot

9. The cockroach breathes:
   A. Through its mouth.   B. Through its nose.
   C. Through its sides.   D. Through its eyes.

Name: _____ Date: _____

Insects: Cockroaches (cont.)

10. Some people eat cockroaches fried in oil and garlic as:
    A. Good luck for the new year.   B. A sign of wealth.
    C. A cure for indigestion.   D. A cure for arthritis.

11. If you see a white or very pale cockroach, it probably means that the cockroach:
    A. Is an albino.   B. Is from Antarctica.
    C. Has shed its skin.   D. Is old.

12. How much of its time does a cockroach spend resting?
    A. 25%   B. 50%
    C. 75%   D. 90%

13. Which of the following is *not* a name for the cockroach?
    A. Shiner   B. Johnny-come-lately
    C. Steam-bug   D. Stream-fly

14. About how many species of pest roaches are native to America?
    A. 0   B. 1,000
    C. 100   D. 2,000

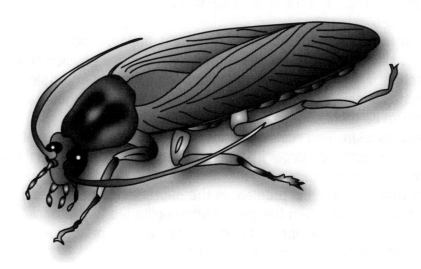

Insects: Cockroaches—Answers

1. **D. Die of thirst.** Cockroaches are capable of living for up to a week without their heads. Eventually, they will die, because without their heads, they can't drink water. They usually die of thirst before they starve to death. The cockroach has a diffused nervous system. The nerve cells are distributed throughout the cockroach, so it is still able to survive for a time without its head.

2. **D. The woods.** Only about one percent of cockroaches are considered pests to humans. Most cockroaches live in warm, tropical habitats and spend their days scavenging on living and dead plant and animal material. American and German cockroaches live in people's homes and eat garbage and kitchen scraps.

3. **B. Hisses.** The Madagascar hissing cockroach is not considered a pest and is kept as a pet by many people. It is wingless and bears live young.

4. **A. Yankee settlers.** In Sweden, cockroaches are called *brotaetare*, which means "bread-eater."

5. **C. To shun the light.** Cockroaches are **nocturnal**, which means they are more active at night. While a person may see a cockroach during the daylight, it is more often seen at night when a person turns on a light and observes it scurrying across the floor.

6. **A. Crazy bug.**

7. **B. TV cockroach.** Cockroaches can adapt to almost any environment, and they eat almost anything—food, hair, soap, tobacco, paint, and glue, to name just a few. The brown-banded cockroach is also known as the TV cockroach because it lives in the back of TV sets and similar appliances. It is a warm habitat, and there is food; that is, if you don't mind eating glue, insulation, and other TV parts.

8. **B. One-foot.** It is six inches long.

9. **C. Through its sides**. Along the sides of a cockroach's body are tiny holes called spiracles. Oxygen enters the cockroach through these holes and follows the tiny breathing tubes called tracheae to all of the cockroach's body parts. A cockroach can hold its breath for 40 minutes.

10. **C. A cure for indigestion.** For centuries, cooked, boiled, ground, and raw, the cockroach has been used as a possible cure for many illnesses and physical disorders. A squashed cockroach applied to a bee sting is supposed to relieve the pain. A tea brewed from cockroaches is said to be a treatment for a disease called generalized edema, sometimes known as dropsy.

11. **C. Has shed its skin.** The cockroach doesn't have an interior skeleton, but a hard exoskeleton. As it becomes larger inside, the outer skeleton remains the same. It would be like a person being required to wear the same shoes and clothes as he or she grew. The cockroach solves this problem in the same way other insects and snakes do—it sheds its outer layer. Then the exoskeleton splits along the back, and the cockroach climbs out. When this happens, the cockroach is very pale or white. A few hours later, a new exoskeleton has hardened and becomes brown.

12. **C. 75%.**

13. **B. Johnny-come-lately.**

14. **A. 0.** Like humans, all pest roaches were immigrants. They might be considered illegal immigrants because they stowed away aboard the ships of explorers and settlers.

Name: _____ Date: _____

Amazing Insect Fact

Directions: Do you want to learn a fascinating fact about an insect? It is hidden in the list of words at the bottom of the page. Read each statement and then cross out the word that applies to the statement in the list below. Once all of the extra words are eliminated, unscramble the remaining words to make a sentence that reveals an amazing insect fact. Write the sentence on your own paper

1. This is the heaviest insect. It weighs $3\frac{1}{2}$ ounces and is 5 inches long.
2. The loudest insects are male _____.
3. The three parts of an insect
4. The stage of development between the larval stage and the adult stage of an insect
5. A scientist who studies insects
6. The biggest insect to have ever lived
7. People have sometimes mistaken dragonflies for _____.
8. Social, wood-eating insects
9. This is the larval stage of moths and butterflies (order *Lepidoptera*). They are like worms but have hair on their bodies.
10. The thin, tubular, protruding mouth part on a butterfly
11. These eat every animal in their path.
12. This insect migrates over 2,000 miles from August to October, flying from Canada and the United States to southern California and central Mexico.
13. The strongest animal relative to its size
14. Produce honey
15. It is possible to determine the approximate outdoor temperature by counting the chirps of a _____.
16. An envelope mainly of silk in which an insect larva forms
17. The change from a larva to an adult insect
18. The largest insect order
19. A hard outer skeleton
20. The only place where insects are not commonly found is in the _____.
21. The most dangerous insect
22. _____ and _____ belong to the second-largest order of insects.
23. The blood of most insects is colorless, green, or _____.
24. These insects are born pregnant and can give birth 10 days after being born themselves.
25. Most of the bees in hives are _____.
26. The most common household insect problem

a, a, a, abdomen, ants, aphids, army ants, bees, butterflies, caterpillars, cicadas, cockroach, cocoon, Coleoptera, cricket, custom, entomologist, Europe, exoskeleton, fairies, Goliath beetle, head, home, in, into, it, metamorphosis, monarch butterfly, mosquito, moths, new, ocean, once, prehistoric dragonfly, proboscis, pupal, release, rhinoceros beetle, termites, thorax, to, was, workers, yellow

Answer: _____

Name: _____ Date: _____

Plants: General

Plants are one of the major kingdoms of living things. The kingdoms are **animalia**, which is made up of animals; **plantae**, which is made up of plants; **protista**, which is made up of mostly single-celled creatures invisible to the human eye that have characteristics of both plants and animals; **fungi**, which is made up of mushrooms, mold, yeast, lichen, etc.; and **monera**, which is made up of bacteria. Plants are important to humans because they give us food, clothing, shelter, and medicine. The study of plants is called **botany**.

1. The compass plant was given its name because:
   A. It looks like a compass.   B. The leaves point north and south.
   C. When the stem floats, it points north. D. It grows on the north side of an oak.

2. Another name for the *titan arum*, an enormous flower, is:
   A. Gargantua.   B. Corpse flower.
   C. Umbrella plant.   D. Dinosaur flower.

3. The Saguaro cactus, found in the southwestern United States, does not grow branches until it is:
   A. 10 years old.   B. 40 years old.
   C. 65 years old.   D. 110 years old.

4. Spanish moss is a member of this family:
   A. Fungus   B. Moss
   C. Pineapple   D. Parasite

5. For which of the following has Spanish moss *not* been used?
   A. Stuffing car seats   B. Stuffing mattresses
   C. Making wigs   D. Medicine

6. Bamboo is a:
   A. Tree.   B. Grass.
   C. Shrub.   D. Parasite.

7. Bamboo grows at a rate of:
   A. 3.3 feet an hour.   B. 3.3 feet a day.
   C. 3.3 feet a week.   D. 3.3 feet a month.

8. What poisonous weed is named after a historic American village?
   A. Bostonia   B. Phillyroot
   C. Jimsonweed   D. Salemwort

Name: _____ Date: _____

Plants: General (cont.)

9. What plant's name means *lion's tooth* in French?
   A. Dandelion
   B. Hound's tooth
   C. Fleur-de-lis
   D. Jonquil

10. What are inky cap, sulphur top, shaggy mane, slimy gomphidius, and pig's ears?
    A. Mushrooms
    B. Herbs
    C. Weeds
    D. Tropical plants

11. What plant has the most species on Earth?
    A. Begonia
    B. Rose
    C. Orchid
    D. Dandelion

12. Mushrooms are:
    A. Fruits.
    B. Vegetables.
    C. Weeds.
    D. Fungi.

13. Which of the following is classified as a grass?
    A. Corn
    B. Wheat
    C. Rye
    D. Oats

Plants: General—Answers

1. **B. The leaves point north and south.** The compass plant grows to between five and ten feet tall and produces flowers that are two to five inches wide. Although it looks similar to a sunflower, the seeds for the compass flower grow where the petals were, not in the center. The large leaves at the bottom of the compass plant almost always align themselves with north and south. Early Americans were aware of this marvel of nature and would look for this plant to give them direction as they traveled.

2. **B. Corpse flower.** *Titan arum* can grow to a height of over six feet or more and opens to a diameter of three to four feet. But the size of the flower is not its most interesting feature. Its odor is. Instead of emitting a pleasant aroma as many flowers do, it gives off a smell so bad that people say it smells like rotting meat. Why does it smell so bad? It does so in order to survive. A flower is the reproductive structure of flowering plants. Many flowers in nature have evolved to attract animals to pollinate the flower. Those that have evolved to attract bees, bats, and other pollinators smell pleasant. The corpse flower, however, is pollinated by carrion beetles, flies, and dung beetles.

3. **C. 65 years old.** The Saguaro cactus, the state flower of Arizona, is found in the southwestern United States. A full-grown saguaro is usually more than 35 feet tall and is slow-growing. It does not flower until it is about 40 years old and does not develop an arm (branch) until it is about 65 years old. It is considered mature when it is 85 years old and may live for 200 years. The saguaro is one of the largest cacti in the southwestern United States and is so rare that it is considered endangered. It is protected within Saguaro National Park.

4. **C. Pineapple.** Spanish moss is a native, perennial plant. It is neither Spanish, nor moss, nor a parasite, as many people think. It is a long, thin, bluish-gray flowering plant that is a member of the pineapple family and lives on tree branches for support. It does not have roots but gets its food and moisture from rainfall and airborne nutrients. In spite of the fact that the plant does not attach itself to trees, the moss will grow only on trees. Sometimes it is seen on telephone poles, fences, or buildings; however, when that happens it is because it has either blown or fallen there. Spanish moss usually doesn't harm the trees upon which it hangs, except when it is wet, Then it can absorb so much water, it gets too heavy and can break the branch on which it hangs.

   Spanish moss can be found in the United States from Virginia all the way down to Argentina in South America. It is sometimes called Florida moss, southern moss, long moss, graybeard, air-plant, old man's beard, and grandfather's whiskers. Native Americans called it tree hair. French explorers called it Spanish beard, while the Spanish called it French hair.

5. **C. Making wigs.** Spanish moss has been used for so many purposes that it is impossible to name them all. It was used by Henry Ford as a seat stuffing for his original Model T automobiles. It was also used as stuffing for mattresses until it was learned that insects infested the plant and caused itching and insect bites. Here is a list of other ways in which Spanish moss has been used: for clothes; fodder for livestock; kindling for fires; when mixed with mud, it was mortar for building; mulch for gardens; to fill potholes; floor mats; to strengthen clay; ropes; horse blankets; food; and medicine. Native Americans

Plants: General—Answers

used it to make fire arrows and to stuff balls that were used in games they played. Today, commercially grown Spanish moss is treated in processors that kill insects and clean and dry the plant. It is used for crafts, braids, saddle blankets, stuffing furniture, and packing material.

6. **B. Grass.** Bamboo is a versatile plant that grows in a lot of different climates. It is found on all of the continents except Antarctica. The advantage bamboo has over other plants is its strength and flexibility. While it will bend in a strong wind, it does not usually break. In fact, its strength when bending is better than thin steel. Bamboo is considered the strongest woody plant on Earth. In spite of the fact that it is a woody plant and can grow as tall as a tree, it is really a type of grass.

7. **B. 3.3 feet a day.** People sometimes say that bamboo grows so fast that one can almost see it grow. While this is an exaggeration, bamboo is the world's tallest grass. It can grow over three feet in a single day. Some species grow over 100 feet tall. There are types of bamboo that will die after fruiting; some do not flower until they are about 30 years old. A remarkable fact concerning flowering is that all the bamboo of a particular species will flower at exactly the same time, no matter where they are located.

8. **C. Jimsonweed.** Jimsonweed, which is a corruption of its original name, Jamestown weed, was named for Jamestown, Virginia. Many of the first colonists in North America were educated and cultured. Soon, however, many other immigrants came to America who were illiterate and had little or no schooling. Some of these later immigrants were farmers and hunters who would encounter animals and plants with which they were not familiar, so they gave them names associated with their appearance, sound, or location. Some examples are bullfrog, lightning bug, razorback, and Jamestown weed. Over time, the Jamestown weed became Jimsonweed.

9. **A. Dandelion.** In French, the dandelion is called *dente de lion*. It was named because of the toothlike points on its leaves.

10. **A. Mushrooms.**

11. **C. Orchid.** The orchid, which is a member of the asparagus family, is truly a remarkable plant. It is the most diverse plant family in nature and includes 20,000 to 30,000 species. This is about 10 percent of all flowering plant species. Some have flowers that are the size of a mosquito, while others are as large as plates. Another unique feature of the orchid is the size of the seeds. They are so small that it would take 1.25 million orchid seeds to weigh one gram. Recent research has indicated that orchids are among the oldest plant families that exist today.

12. **D. Fungi.** When we think of mushrooms, we usually think of an appetizing food. However, there are thousands of species of mushroom, and the majority of them are bitter, tough, and woody. Some species are poisonous and can cause illness or death.

13. **A, B, C, D.** Most cereal grain plants are types of grass. Incidentally, the term *corn* means different things in different countries. In the United States, *Indian maize* is called *corn*. What we call *oats* is called *corn* in Scotland and Ireland. In England, the term *corn* refers to the grain that those in the United States call *wheat*.

Name: _____ Date: _____

Plants: Trees

Trees are woody plants with a main **trunk,** or **stem**. They are the tallest plants, although some tree species are very short. Trees are **perennial** plants, which means that they live for several seasons. Trees grow almost every place in the world. They live high in the mountains, in very cold regions, and in hot, tropical regions.

Trees are very important to the environment and to humans. They protect the land against **erosion**, which is the wearing away of topsoil due to wind and water. Forests and trees store water that is important for the ecosystem during periods of drought. Removing forests exposes the area to floods and eventually droughts. Forests also furnish protection and food for many plants and animals. They are also important for the climate and atmosphere, since the leaves of trees absorb carbon dioxide in the air and produce oxygen that is necessary for life. In addition, trees provide many products such as lumber, food, chemicals, and drugs.

1. The jungle tree with the nickname "walking palm" was given its name because:
   A. It actually walks.
   B. When the wind blows, it appears to walk.
   C. It is found in the Walking Valley.
   D. It was discovered by Dr. Harold Wakeen.

2. If you make a notch in a tree, as the tree grows the notch will:
   A. Rise higher.
   B. Stay the same distance from the ground.
   C. Sink closer to the ground.
   D. Disappear.

3. The oldest living tree is:
   A. "Methuselah," a bristlecone pine
   B. A Douglas fir called "Socrates."
   C. A redwood named "Eternal God."
   D. A Chinese almond tree named "Chin."

4. How much water does a large deciduous tree use each day?
   A. 1–10 gallons.
   B. 25–50 gallons.
   C. 150–200 gallons.
   D. 300–900 gallons.

5. There is a white oak tree in Athens, Georgia, that is known as:
   A. The tree that lost the war.
   B. The haunted oak.
   C. The tree that owns itself.
   D. The tree that saved Jefferson Davis.

6. Many feel that the Manchineel Tree of the Caribbean coast and the Florida Everglades is the world's:
   A. Most dangerous tree.
   B. Most beautiful tree.
   C. Smelliest tree.
   D. Ugliest tree.

7. One large tree can provide a day's oxygen to this many people.
   A. 24
   B. 4
   C. 14
   D. 40

96

Name: _____   Date: _____

Plants: Trees (cont.)

8. How many mature trees are necessary to absorb the carbon dioxide produced by a typical car each year?
    A. 50   B. 500
    C. 5,000   D. 50,000

9. Although coast redwood trees are cultivated in many places, the tree thrives best when certain conditions are present. Which condition is *not* important for a redwood to reach its fullest potential?
    A. Fog   B. Mild climate
    C. Open area   D. Rich soil

10. During dry summers, the coast redwoods:
    A. Become dormant.   B. Die.
    C. Actually shrink.   D. Create their own rain.

11. How many different kinds of trees are there?
    A. 200   B. 2,000
    C. 20,000   D. 200,000

12. In 1977, a decree was passed in the Philippines that required every person over 10 years old to plant a tree:
    A. On his or her birthday   B. When he or she marries.
    C. When a child is born.   D. Every month for five years.

13. Willow bark was the original source for:
    A. Indigo dye.   B. Aspirin.
    C. Super Glue.   D. Shampoo.

14. Which of the following was *not* considered as a name for the redwood?
    A. Sequoia
    B. Wellingtonea
    C. Gargantua
    D. Americus

15. The banyan tree that grows on the Thomas Edison estate in Fort Myers, Florida, is unusual because:
    A. It takes up almost an acre of ground.
    B. It has no leaves.
    C. It can only exist in pairs.
    D. It only lives one year.

Plants: Trees—Answers

1. **A. It actually walks.** Rainforests are warm, wet forests with tall crowded trees and millions of plants and animals. One would think with all of the rain, trees, plants, and animals, the soil in a rainforest would be very fertile. This isn't true. A tropical rainforest has soil that is only about 3-4 inches thick. There is a thick clay that lies underneath the soil. Most of the nutrients are absorbed into the soil and are leached out by the abundant rainfall. This leaves the soil infertile and acidic. Trees and plants need both nutrients and sunlight to survive. That is why the walking palm moves or "walks." It will send new roots towards areas that are rich in nutrients or that have more sunlight and then sever the old roots. It continues this process its entire life.

2. **B. Stay the same distance from the ground.**

3. **C. A redwood named "Eternal God."** For many years, scientists thought the oldest tree, as well as the oldest living thing on Earth, was a bristlecone pine in the White Mountains of California named "Methuselah." It was thought to be almost 4,800 years old, making it as old as the pyramids. However, the Guinness Book of World Records currently lists a California redwood named "Eternal God" as the oldest tree on Earth. "Eternal God" is 238 feet tall and has a diameter of 19.6 feet. The tree is believed to be 12,000 years old, although some feel it is only 7,000 years old.

4. **D. 300–900 gallons.** A deciduous tree is a tree that sheds its leaves each year when the weather turns cold or when there is a drought. When it is hot and sunny, a large deciduous tree can use 300–900 gallons of water. Some may use even more. Over an entire growing season, a 100-foot deciduous tree can use over 11,000 gallons of water from the soil and then release the moisture into the air. Large trees can lose more than 200 gallons of water from their leaves each day. This provides a cooling effect that some estimate to be the same as air-conditioning twelve rooms for a growing season. A shade tree positioned on the west side of a home can keep the home 20 percent cooler than a home without such a tree.

5. **C. The tree that owns itself.** It is reported that a deed granted in 1820 by Col. William H. Jackson, a professor at the University of Georgia, willed ownership of a white oak tree to itself. In addition to owning itself, the tree was granted possession of the 64 square feet of land on which the white oak grew. The deed was granted in the Colonel's will to protect the beloved oak. However, in 1952 the original tree blew down during a storm, so citizens of Athens planted another, grown from one of the original tree's acorns. The story of the tree that owns itself first appeared in the Athens Weekly Banner on August 12, 1890. It has been repeated since. It also appeared in the famous newspaper column called Ripley's "Believe It or Not."

6. **A. Most dangerous tree.** Many plants have devised ways in which to protect themselves. Most pose more than just a little discomfort to humans. This is not true of the deadly Manchineel trees. Found on the Caribbean coast and in the Florida Everglades, the Manchineel secretes a poisonous acid sap. When this sap comes into contact with the skin, itching and blisters occur. The sap is not water-soluble and cannot be easily washed off. Then, when the victim scratches the blister, the poison is transferred to the fingertips and other parts of the body. When the sap comes into contact with the eye, a person can be blinded. Eating its fruit causes blistering and severe pain.

Plants: Trees—Answers (cont.)

7. **B. 4.**

8. **B. 500.**

9. **C. Open area.** The coast redwoods are the tallest living species on Earth. They can reach heights of 300–350 feet and have diameters that range from 16–18 feet. Coast redwoods grow very quickly. Under the right conditions, young redwoods can grow more than six feet in a single growing season. They also have a very long life.

    The composition of the redwood is unique. Its bark is very thick, as much as a foot thick. When redwood is exposed to fire, it chars and becomes a heat shield. The wood resists termites, ants, and other pests, so it is sometimes used as the first layer of boards in a wall. Redwood is also resistant to water rot.

    The coastal redwood tree (*Sequoia sempervirens*) achieves its great heights and luxuriant groves in the only place in the world that meets all of the conditions that enable it to thrive. That place is a 450-mile strip along the Pacific coast of North America. The climate is mild, and there is moisture year-round because of the rain in the winter and fog in the summer. The trees live in an area with rich soil, and they are sheltered.

10. **D. Create their own rain.** Redwoods use moisture very efficiently. They take in a lot of their water from the air, through their needles. Of course, they take in water from their roots and are able to siphon the moisture up the great heights of the tree. During dry summers, the coast redwoods create their own rain by condensing fog into rain to provide moisture for the roots of the trees

11. **C. 20,000.**

12. **D. Every month for five years.** This is called the Philippine Reforestation Program. Those who violate the law lose their citizens' rights and can be fined $175. The seedlings are provided by the government. The purpose of the law is to plant 360 million saplings per year and reduce the country's deforestation.

13. **B. Aspirin.** Various medicines have been created from thousands of plant species, but the medicine made from willow bark has probably been used more than any other. Willow is the original source of aspirin. Now aspirin can be easily made by other methods. The ancient Greeks and Europeans chewed leaves of willow in order to reduce pain. Possibly even before the ancient Greeks, North American Indians used willow to relieve pain and fever. The same is true of Hottentots in southern Africa.

14. **C. Gargantua.** The redwood was named for Sequoia to honor the great Cherokee, the only human to create a written language alone. Other names that were used before the name Sequoia were "Wellingtonea," in honor of the Duke of Wellington and "Americus."

15. **A. It takes up almost an acre of ground.** There are several different types and sizes of banyans. The Edison banyan is the third largest in the world. Unlike most trees, the banyan roots sprout from branches. The roots drop to the ground and form a prop for the limbs. Eventually, these roots become a firm part of the tree.

Name: _____   Date: _____

Plants: Fruits and Vegetables

People generally think they know the difference between fruits and vegetables. Those that taste sweet or sour are generally considered to be fruits, while plants that are not sugary are considered to be vegetables. To a scientist who studies plants, this definition is not accurate. In general, **vegetables** are defined as plants cultivated for their edible parts. They have a soft, not woody, stem. Vegetables can be grouped according to the edible part of each plant: leaves (lettuce), stalks (celery), roots (radishes), bulbs (onions), tubers (potatoes), and flowers (broccoli). On the other hand, the term "fruit" has a more specific meaning.

Fruit, which is an excellent source of food, vitamins, and minerals, is the seed-bearing object of a flowering plant. Fruit is a ripened part of the flower's female reproductive anatomy. While the fleshy, sweet-tasting fruits, such as peaches, apples, and plums, are familiar to us, the term "fruit" is really a more general term that includes dry fruits, such as almonds and acorns. While it may be hard to believe, grains of rice, corn, and wheat are also considered dry fruits. Some foods we usually think of as vegetables are also classified as fruits. These include tomatoes, peppers, and eggplant. Why are they fruits? Because they develop from the female part of a flower.

1. During every game, Babe Ruth, the famous baseball player, would do something unusual. He would:
   A. Put a cabbage leaf under his cap.   B.   Eat a raw onion.
   C. Put a lucky buckeye nut in its pocket. D.   Wear a necklace of garlic.

2. A small biotech firm in Denmark has genetically engineered watercress plants to:
   A. Become a fuel for automobiles.   B.   Fight cancer.
   C. Find buried landmines.   D.   Remove wrinkles.

3. A small cluster of about 20 bananas is called a:
   A. Bunch.   B.   Hand.
   C. Crowd.   D.   Gathering.

4. In colonial America, stores who sold candies and sweets would sometimes rent these:
   A. Fruit dryers   B.   Bananas
   C. Pineapples   D.   Dried mangos

5. In the 1700s–1800s, this was symbol of hospitality:
   A. Apple   B.   Peach
   C. Banana   D.   Pineapple

6. Which of the following is a member of the rose family?
   A. Almonds   B.   Peaches
   C. Sweetbrier   D.   Cherries

Name: _____ Date: _____

Plants: Fruits and Vegetables (cont.)

7. What is the name of the white fibrous membrane inside the skin and around the sections of citrus fruit?
   A. Rag
   B. Sheet
   C. Snow
   D. The white fiber inside the skin

8. Which country or state is the largest producer of bananas?
   A. India
   B. Costa Rica
   C. Hawaii
   D. Ecuador

9. Which of the following is not a true berry?
   A. Strawberry
   B. Raspberry
   C. Blackberry
   D. Eggplant

10. The avocado was once called the:
    A. Leather fruit.
    B. Alligator pear.
    C. Mexican kernel.
    D. Palm seed.

11. The banana is a:
    A. Fruit.
    B. Vegetable.
    C. Herb.
    D. Flower.

12. Which is *not* a member of the lily family?
    A. Onion
    B. Garlic
    C. Aster
    D. Asparagus

13. Important in the manufacturing of dynamite is/are:
    A. Beans.
    B. Peanuts.
    C. Coffee.
    D. Tobacco.

14. Arnold Bly became famous when he inscribed the Lord's Prayer on:
    A. A mountain in South Dakota.
    B. The Statue of Liberty.
    C. A grain of rice.
    D. A mosque in Baghdad.

Plants: Fruits and Vegetables—Answers

1. **A. Put a cabbage leaf under his cap.** Babe Ruth would wear a cabbage leaf under his cap in order to keep cool during those long baseball games. He would change it every two innings in order to keep it fresh.

2. **C. Find buried landmines.** Landmines are devices designed to explode when triggered by pressure or a tripwire. They are usually hidden on or just below the surface of the ground. The purpose of mines when used by soldiers is to kill or hurt an enemy soldier or destroy his vehicle. After a war is over, the locations of landmines are often forgotten, and anyone unlucky enough to come into contact with one may be either killed or maimed. While the use of landmines was outlawed in the 1997 Ottawa Convention, One-World International estimates that there are still more than 80 million hidden landmines located in 70 countries around the world. These landmines have killed or maimed more than one million people since 1975. Each year, another 25,000 victims are added to this total. This is why the Aresa Biodetection Company has genetically engineered the thale cress plant, which is normally bright green, to turn red when it detects even slight amounts of nitrogen dioxide leaking from buried landmines. Landmines are cheaply made and often leak. The cress seeds would be sown by sprayers or crop dusters.

3. **B. Hand.** Bananas are mature about three months after they flower. While on the plant, the fruit seems to be growing upside down. A bunch of bananas weighs between 80 and 125 pounds. Each bunch has about 15 "hands," or rows. Each hand has about 20 bananas. These individual bananas are called "fingers." The word *banana* comes from the Arabic *banan*, which means "finger."

4. **C. Pineapples.** Since pineapples were imported, they were rare in the colonies. They were expensive, and housewives wanted to have them on display in their homes. Having a pineapple was not only a sign that a family was wealthy enough to purchase a pineapple, but that the housewife was influential enough to get it. Stores who sold sweets would sometimes rent pineapples to households to be displayed in a home. Those renting the pineapple would invite friends and neighbors into the house in the hope the guests would notice the pineapple and be impressed. Of course, the hostess would not want her guests to realize the fruit was only rented. When the pineapple was returned to the store owner, he would sell it to someone who was wealthier.

5. **D. Pineapple.** Pineapples, which are grown in the tropics, were unknown to Europeans until Christopher Columbus and his men tasted this sweet, delicious fruit on their second voyage in the Caribbean area. In Colonial America, pineapples were rarities, brought to the colonies by seafaring captains and sailors. Fresh pineapples were expensive and served to special guests as a dessert. When a seafaring captain arrived home from a voyage, he would put a fresh pineapple by his front door on the gatepost to announce to everyone that he was home and that guests could visit. Eventually, the pineapple took on a symbolic meaning in colonial America. It was known as a universal symbol of hospitality and welcome.

6. **A, B, C, D.** Many people do not know that the rose family of plants includes not only flowers but apples, pears, plums, cherries, almonds, peaches, and apricots.

Plants: Fruits and Vegetables—Answers (cont.)

7. **A. Rag.**

8. **A. India.** It is estimated that about 90 percent of the world's bananas and plantains are grown on small farms and consumed locally. Plantains are a type of banana plant. They are more starchy and not as sweet as regular bananas and must be cooked before being eaten. India is the largest producer of bananas, and Uganda is the largest producer of plantains. About half of the world's bananas are grown in Asia, and almost 75 percent of the world's plantains are grown in Africa. It is estimated that 20 million people eat bananas or plantains as their major source of dietary carbohydrate. This is especially true in east Africa, where bananas and plantains constitute the main staple food for about half of the population. Most of the world's bananas and plantains grown for export come from Latin America and the Caribbean.

9. **A, B, C.** In many cases the fruits that we refer to as berries are not true berries. To botanists, however, a berry is a fleshy fruit that contains one or more seeds and develops from a single ovary in a plant. By this definition, true berries include tomatoes, peppers, eggplants, persimmons, and grapes. For reasons that involve fruit reproduction, raspberries, blackberries, and strawberries are not true berries, but are called aggregate fruits.

10. **B. Alligator pear.** The word *avocado* is a corruption of the Spanish word "aguacate" which means alligator. It was given that name because people thought the trees grew in areas inhabited by alligators.

11. **A, C.** A banana, that yellow thing you buy at the store, peel, and eat is obviously a fruit. But the plant that produces the banana is an herb. An herb is a plant without a woody stem; it usually dies back at the end of each growing season. (Incidentally, the word *herb* can be pronounced with or without the "h" sound.) Banana plants are not trees. They are the largest plants on Earth that do not have a woody stem, so they are technically giant herbs of the same family as lilies and orchids. Banana plants die after fruiting like all herbs do. Bananas are America's most popular fruit and are a good source of vitamin C, potassium, and dietary fiber.

12. **C. Aster.** The lily family is a large family of plants, *Liliaceae*, that has showy flowers usually producing bulbs or rhizomes. Almost everything in the lily subfamily is edible, such as onions, garlic, and blue camas. But there are some deadly plants in the family that could easily be mistaken for edible lilies. So it is important to harvest lilies for food **only** if you can positively identify them. A subfamily of the lily is the asparagus. It produces berries instead of dry seed capsules.

13. **B. Peanuts.** Dynamite is an explosive made from nitroglycerin. Nitroglycerin is a chemical compound obtained by nitrating glycerol. Glycerin, also called glycerine and glycerol, is made from peanut oil. Peanut oil comes from peanuts.

14. **C. A grain of rice.** It is also reported that he was able to write legibly on a strand of human hair. He demonstrated his lettering ability at the 1939 World's Fair in New York.

Name: _____   Date: _____

Puzzle: "The Year There Was No Summer"

    There was a period between 1811 and 1817 when a temporary climatic cooling took place. The year most affected was 1816. In the United States, New England experienced the worst of the cold weather. During the summer, frost and freezing temperatures were common. Frost killed most of the crops that had been planted. There were two large snowstorms in June. On the fourth of July, people wore heavy overcoats. In July and August, ice formed on lakes and rivers as far south as Pennsylvania. The cold temperature resulted in failed crops; as a result, many people from New England moved to the Midwest.

    What caused this cold weather in the summer, which was also experienced in Canada, Europe, and Asia? Many scientists believe it was partially caused by the volcanic eruptions of Mount Tambora on the island of Sumbawa, which is now part of Indonesia. The eruption sent over one and a half million metric tons of dust into the upper atmosphere. The dust blocked the sun's radiation, causing the temperature to drop. People in New England called 1816 "The Year There Was No Summer" and the "Poverty Year." But others had a more colorful name for this period. The answer can be found in the puzzle below. Follow the directions on the following page.

E	M	U	Q	L	K	N	K	X	C
H	I	H	T	Y	G	F	L	P	D
I	V	E	Z	U	Q	A	F	J	R
D	W	B	X	O	E	T	S	R	S
M	A	E	D	L	Q	K	U	P	Y
J	Z	P	R	O	X	C	V	J	W
V	C	H	S	A	T	B	G	E	I
W	K	R	Y	A	Q	M	T	E	V
B	F	S	F	H	J	U	D	L	X
N	B	Z	N	U	G	I	P	O	L

Answer: __ __ __   __ __ __ __ __   __ __ __ __ __ __ __

           1   2   3   4   5   6   7   8   9 10 11 12 13 14 15

   __ __ __   __ __ __ __ __   __ __ __ __ __ __ __

  16 17 18   19 20 21 22 23   24 25   26 27 28 29 30

Name: _____ Date: _____

 Directions: "The Year There Was No Summer"

Directions: Using the grid on the preceding page, learn what some people called this unusually cold period. Write the letters on the corresponding blanks on the previous page.

1. Pick the letter that is between the letters V and Z.
2. Pick the letter above V and below W.
3. Pick the letter that is below a V and above a T.
4. Pick the letter between C and S.
5. Pick the letter that is one level above and one box to the right of the Q and one level above the K.
6. Pick the letter that is diagonally between the letter Z and the letter X.
7. Pick the letter that is the farthest away from the letter that has no letter to its right or below it.
8. Pick the letter that is the farthest to the left and farthest down on the grid.
9. Pick the letter between F and J.
10. In the first line of the grid is the name of a flightless bird found in Australia. Pick the last letter in its name.
11. Pick the letter between two K's.
12. Pick the letter that is diagonally between P and O.
13. Pick the letter that is in the fourth line and only has one letter to its right.
14. Pick the letter located between the two Q's.
15. Pick the letter that is diagonally between the letters M and O.
16. Pick the letter that has its twin above it and a Q to its right.
17. Pick the letter that has the letter B two spaces to the left and the letter G two spaces to the right.
18. There is a word hidden in the first down column. Choose the last letter of that word.
19. There is a word hidden in the seventh down column. Choose the first letter of that word.
20. Pick the letter that is two spaces above the letter Z and two spaces below the letter P.
21. There is a man's name in the fifth column. Pick the middle letter of that name.
22. Pick the letter that has the letter Q two above it and two to the right of it.
23. Pick the letter that is between the ninth letter of the alphabet and the seventh letter of the alphabet.
24. Pick the letter that lies diagonally between two U's.
25. Pick the letter that has no letter below it and only one letter to its right.
26. Pick the letter that has only one letter above it and a P to the left.
27. Pick the letter two to the right of the letter I and two to the left of the letter U.
28. Pick the letter in the seventh column that is the middle letter of a word.
29 Pick the letter that has the letters A, M, C, and O at its points.
30. Pick the eighth letter of the alphabet that is two above the letter B.

Name: _____ Date: _____

The Universe

Our **solar system** consists of the sun and everything that orbits it. This includes the eight planets and their satellites, as well as minor planets, comets, and asteroids. The center of this solar system is the sun, a star of average size and brightness. The light from the sun is produced by the sun's ability to turn hydrogen into helium. The solar system includes eight major planets. Scientists divide these planets into two groups. The **inner planets** are Mars, Earth, Venus, and Mercury. These are small planets that are mainly composed of rock and iron. Neptune, Uranus, Saturn, and Jupiter are referred to as the **outer planets** and are larger and composed mainly of hydrogen, helium,

and ice. Pluto has been classified as a minor planet. Pluto is *usually* farther from the sun than any of the other eight planets. Because of its unusual orbit, it is sometimes *closer* to the sun than Neptune. In addition to the planets, there are many smaller celestial bodies. Asteroids are small rocky bodies that move in orbits mainly between the orbits of Mars and Jupiter. Comets are composed of gas and dust and orbit the sun.

1. In 1910, when it was announced that Halley's Comet would once again pass the earth, people in Europe:
   A. Bought anti-comet pills.   B. Thought the world would end.
   C. Thought aliens were coming.   D. Expected God to arrive.

2. A comet is:
   A. Molten rock.   B. Molten metal.   C. A small meteor.   D. A giant snowball.

3. How long does it take for light from the sun to reach the earth?
   A. 30 seconds   B. 1 minute   C. 8 minutes   D. 30 minutes

4. During a lunar eclipse, the moon:
   A. Disappears.   B. Appears to turn red.
   C. Appears to turn blue.   D. Appears to blink on and off.

5. Many scientists think _____ killed the dinosaurs.
   A. The Ice Age   B. Sunspots   C. An asteroid   D. Cavemen

6. Eratosthenes was a Greek astronomer, mathematician, and poet who lived in the third century B.C. He was able to:
   A. Measure the radius of Earth   B. Prove the Earth was round
   C. Calculate the distance to the moon   D. Discover Mars

Name: _____ Date: _____

The Universe (cont.)

7. A year on Pluto takes _____ Earth-years.
    A. 2.47   B. 24.77   C. 247.7   D. 2477.7

8. Mars is called the "red planet" because:
    A. It is rusty.   B. It has copper deposits.
    C. Eric the Red used it to navigate.   D. Its atmosphere makes it look red.

9. Which of the following has Venus *not* been called?
    A. Morning star   B. Evening star
    C. Second planet from the sun   D. Aphrodite

10. Which one of the following is *most* important for life as we know it to have evolved on Earth?
    A. Air   B. Water   C. Circular orbit of Earth D. Seasons

11. When humans first observed Jupiter's Southern Hemisphere 400 years ago, they discovered Jupiter's Great Red Spot, twice the size of Earth. The Great Red Spot is still there today, but over the years, it has changed shape, size, and color. Scientists now believe that Jupiter's Great Red Spot is:
    A. A sea of gas.   B. A hurricane.
    C. Iron oxide (rust).   D. An illusion caused by the atmosphere.

12. We know the earth is turning on its axis. How fast do you think the earth is rotating?
    A. 1 mile an hour   B. 10 miles an hour
    C. 100 miles an hour   D. 1,000 miles an hour

13. A "shooting star" is about the size of a:
    A. Grain of sand.   B. Basketball.   C. Automobile.   D. House.

14. What is a blue moon?
    A. A full moon   B. A quarter moon
    C. A lunar eclipse   D. The second full moon in a month

15. When pulsars were discovered in 1967, the astronomers originally called them LGM, which stood for:
    A. Little Green Men.   B. Low Grade Millibars.
    C. Latent Gravitational Magnetism.   D. Light Gamma Matter.

16. The planet Uranus was originally called:
    A. Zeus.   B. George.   C. Galileo.   D. Poseidon.

17. Venus and Uranus are the only two planets that:
    A. Are larger than Earth.   B. Are made of molten metal.
    C. Do not have an atmosphere.   D. Rotate clockwise.

The Universe—Answers

1. **A. Bought anti-comet pills.** Halley's Comet orbits the sun in a direction opposite to that of the planets and can be seen from the earth once in about every 76 years. The comet, which was named for the English astronomer Edmond Halley, was observed and recorded as early as 239 B.C. by the Chinese. In ancient times, people thought comets had special meanings; they were usually a bad omen. Wars, epidemics, and natural disasters are common, but if a comet appeared close to one of these catastrophes, people thought it was related. Over the years, some people tied Halley's Comet  to certain terrible events. The fall of Jerusalem occurred in 66 A.D. Rome was sacked by the Huns in 373 A.D. In 1066, there was the battle of Hastings. These events all happened when Halley's Comet was visible from Earth. So when the announcement of the arrival of Halley's Comet was made in 1910, people in Europe became hysterical. They expected some terrible calamity to happen. Some hid in the forests; others killed themselves. There were even newspaper articles that quoted scientists' claims that the comet's tail contained a deadly cloud of poison that would kill those who were exposed to it. Enterprising businessmen sold "anti-comet pills," which were guaranteed to protect those who took them from the comet's poisonous fumes. People eagerly bought the pills, and apparently they worked because no one was poisoned by the comet. Of course, those who didn't take them weren't poisoned, either.

2. **D. A giant snowball.** A comet is small compared to other heavenly bodies. Many scientists refer to comets as "dirty snowballs" or "dirty icebergs" that revolve around the sun. Actually, comets are mostly composed of frozen gases such as water vapor, carbon dioxide, and methane. When a comet is far from the sun, it is cold, and its material is frozen solid. When a comet nears the sun, however, the gases heat up, and they develop tails of luminous material often visible from the earth.

3. **C. 8 minutes.** The sun is 93 million miles away from Earth, so by the time the light reaches Earth, the light is eight minutes old.

4. **B. Appears to turn red.** A lunar eclipse occurs about every six months when the earth passes between the sun and the moon, and the earth's shadow passes over the moon. Sometimes the shadow falls on only part of the moon, but at other times, it covers the moon completely. The earth's shadow on the moon is not dark gray as one would expect; it ranges in color from dark brown and red to bright orange and sometimes even yellow. However, red is the most common color. This phenomenon is caused by the earth's atmosphere. As the sunlight passes through the earth's atmosphere, the blue light is filtered out, and the remaining light is red or orange in color. This is similar to the way in which a simple lens or prism bends light. Lunar eclipses are safe to watch. There is no need for any type of eye protection.

5. **C. An asteroid.** Scientists believe a huge asteroid, from four to nine miles in diameter, slammed into the earth about 65 million years ago and led to the extinction of the dino-

The Universe—Answers (cont.)

saurs. Scientists think the asteroid hit the earth near what is now known as the Yucatán Peninsula in Mexico and left a crater 120 miles wide. The impact collision caused huge fires, tsunamis, and storms and threw dust and debris into the atmosphere, blocking the sun for several months. Temperatures around the world fell, and large amounts of sulfuric acid in the air burned the ground. Once the dust settled, the temperature rose dramatically. As the air cleared, the carbon dioxide left over from the explosion created a greenhouse effect, which caused the temperatures to soar for centuries. Plants died, and animals starved to death. It is estimated about 90 percent of all animal species on Earth became extinct. Dinosaurs were the chief casualty of this calamity.

6. **A. Measure the radius of Earth.** Without the use of precision instruments, his calculations came within 1 percent of the value determined by today's technology. How did he do it? Geometry. He used a formula that involved measuring the altitude of the noontime sun on June 21st. A full explanation of how he did it can be found at *(http://astrosun2. astro.cornell.edu/academics/courses//astro201/eratosthenes.htm)* and other locations on the Internet.

7. **C. 247.7.** Each Pluto-day is equivalent to 6.39 Earth-days. It takes 247.7 Earth-years for Pluto to orbit the sun once, making a Pluto-year equivalent to 247.7 Earth-years. Mercury has a year that is only 88 Earth-days long. Jupiter has a day and night only nine hours, 54 minutes long, giving it the shortest day and night of any of the planets. One Earth-day (and night) is 24 hours long.

8. **A. It is rusty.** Mars appears red because it is rusting. The red color of the planet comes from the iron and iron oxide called **rust**.

9. **D. Aphrodite.** Aphrodite was the Greek goddess of love and beauty. Her Roman name was Venus, but the planet was never called Aphrodite. Venus is the second planet from the sun, and, in some seasons, it is called "evening star." At other times of the year. it is called the "morning star." Mercury is also sometimes called the evening or morning star. Other planets, such as Mars and Jupiter, may also appear as evening or morning stars during points in their orbits.

10. **C. Circular orbit of Earth.** Certainly water and air were important in creating and evolving life on our planet. But even with these two elements present, life, as we know it, would be impossible if it weren't for two factors. The first is the distance the planet is from the sun. The second is its almost perfect circular orbit. If Earth were closer to the sun, the water, which is essential to life, would boil away. If Earth were farther from the sun, the water would freeze into ice, making life as we know it difficult or impossible. For the same reason, a circular orbit is important. Earth's orbit is slightly elliptical, but it is not extreme enough to cause great differences in temperature. If the orbit were more oval shaped, the water would alternately boil as the earth came close to the sun and then freeze as it went far away from the sun. This would make life difficult on Earth.

11. **B. A hurricane.** The Great Red Spot is a storm similar to a hurricane on Earth. It is remarkable because of its size, longevity, and power. Its winds reach speeds as high as 270 miles per hour. Hurricane Katrina, which devastated New Orleans on August 29, 2005, had winds 125 mph when it made landfall near Pearlington, Mississippi.

The Universe—Answers (cont.)

12. **D. 1,000 miles an hour.** When you are standing still, you are actually spinning at about 1,000 miles per hour. At the same time, the earth is moving about our sun at about 67,000 miles per hour. If that isn't enough, our whole solar system is turning around the center of our galaxy at 490,000 miles per hour.

13. **A. Grain of sand.** A shooting star, sometimes called a falling star, has nothing to do with a star. These impressive streaks of light that can be seen in the sky at night are caused by small bits of dust and rock called meteoroids. Once these meteoroids come into contact with Earth's atmosphere, they burn up. There are literally millions of shooting stars each day. Of course, we cannot see the ones that happen during the day because the brightness of the shooting stars is much less than the brightness of the sunlight. At night, we can only see a small area of the sky, so we only see about a dozen shooting stars per hour. Sometimes there are meteor showers where shooting stars can be seen every few minutes.

14. **D. The second full moon in a month.** Two full moons during one calendar month is rare. On average, it occurs about once every two and a half years. So when a person says something happens "once in a blue moon," they mean that it doesn't happen very often.

15. **A. Little Green Men.** The pulsar was discovered in 1967 by Jocelyn Bell and Antony Hewish of the University of Cambridge, England. At first, they did not know what the regular emissions of the pulsar were. They even considered the possibility that the emission might be coming from an extraterrestrial civilization, so they called their discovery, **LGM-1**, for "little green men." Later, their pulsar was called **CP 1919**. It is now referred to as **PSR 1919+21**.

16. **B. George.** Uranus was discovered by the British astronomer Sir William Herschel in 1781. He originally named the planet Georgium Sidus, which means star of George, in honor of his royal patron, King George III of Great Britain. Later, the planet was called Herschel in honor of its discoverer. The German astronomer Johann Elert Bode suggested the name *Uranus*, which was eventually used by others.

17. **D. Rotate clockwise.** From Venus and Uranus, the sun seems to rise in the west and set in the east, which is just the opposite of Earth. Why this is, no one knows for sure. It is thought that perhaps these two planets were hit by a large planetoid, causing the backward rotation. In addition to its clockwise rotation, Uranus rotates on its side.

Name: _____ Date: _____

Physical World

Physics is a branch of science that studies matter and energy and the relation between the two.

1. If a person would shoot a bullet from a rifle that was aimed parallel to the Earth's surface and dropped a bullet at the same time from the same height, the bullet from the rifle would strike the earth:
    A. Shortly after the other bullet.
    B. Long after the other bullet.
    C. Before the other bullet.
    D. At the same time as the other bullet.

2. When an ordinary piece of steel is struck by lightning, it will:
    A. Melt.
    B. Shatter into powder.
    C. Turn into a magnet.
    D. Reflect the lightning.

3. When Ludwig van Beethoven, the great music composer, grew older, he was totally deaf. In order to compose music, he would:
    A. Put his head on the piano.
    B. Put a wooden stick in his teeth.
    C. Put a glass of water on the piano.
    D. Hire a blind woman to help him.

4. Some scientists believe it might be possible to hear sounds made thousands of years ago by:
    A. Examining pottery.
    B. Studying mummies.
    C. Listening to rocks.
    D. Recording sounds in caves.

5. Through which of the following does sound move fastest?
    A. Air.
    B. Cork.
    C. Water.
    D. Steel.

6. If a rubber ball and a steel ball, both the same size, are both thrown with equal force on a hard pavement, the rubber ball will bounce:
    A. Higher than the steel ball.
    B. Not as high as the steel ball.
    C. At the same height as the steel ball.
    D. Sometimes higher, sometimes lower.

7. If you flip a penny 1,000,000 times, it will:
    A. Land on heads most of the time.
    B. Land on tails most of the time.
    C. Land on heads half of the time.
    D. Land on its edge 5% of the time.

8. The sound made from a cracking whip is caused by:
    A. The tip moving faster than sound.
    B. The tip slapping against the whip.
    C. The tip slapping against the air.
    D. The tip slapping against the ground.

9. When dry ice warms up, it becomes:
    A. Water.
    B. Carbon dioxide gas.
    C. Liquid nitrogen.
    D. Freon.

Physical World—Answers

1. **D. At the same time as the other bullet.** When the rifle is shot and the bullet is dropped at the same time, they both are being pulled by gravity. The fact that one is shot and one is dropped makes no difference. The pull of gravity is the same on both. The answer assumes that there is no air resistance and the land over which the rifle is shot is level. If the bullet that is shot travels far enough, the curvature of the earth becomes a factor. If there is a hill in the direction of the bullet, the results would vary.

2. **C. Turn into a magnet.**

3. **B. Put a wooden stick in his teeth.** Ludwig van Beethoven was one of the greatest music composers who ever lived. Although he lived over two hundred years ago, his music is still played every day. What is most remarkable is that much of his composing occurred when he was deaf. His deafness developed gradually and happened at a time in history when there was not much that could be done about it. For several years, Beethoven used an ear trumpet to amplify sounds. An ear trumpet is a device with a small end, which a person puts to his ear, and a large end into which people would talk. As his hearing grew worse, he would talk to someone and then hand them a book to write out their part of the conversation so he could read it. In order to compose music when he was deaf, he would hold a stick between his teeth and put the other end of the stick on the piano. In this way, he could feel the vibrations of the music.

4. **A. Examining pottery.** The phonograph recording invented by Thomas Edison was a machine with a cylinder covered with a soft material such as tin foil, wax, or lead. As the cylinder turned, a stylus drew grooves on its surface, and sound was recorded. The recording could then be played back by having a needle trace the grooves. In order to be heard, the sound needed to be amplified. Some scientists think the potter's wheel is actually a low-grade sound-recording instrument that works just like the methods originally used to make audio recordings. As the wheel turned, and the potter touched the surface of the pot, the sounds around him or her may have accidentally been recorded. This would especially be true if the potter happened to use a sharp metal tool in the final step to smooth the surface. Scientists believe it might be possible to recover the sounds accidentally recorded into the pottery.

5. **D. Steel.** The speed of sound depends on many factors, such as temperature, wind conditions, humidity, and the medium through which it is traveling. Sound waves move energy from one place to another in a chain reaction. Sound travels faster through warm air than through cold air. It travels faster through humid air than dry air. Sound waves also move faster through a denser medium because energy is more easily passed between molecules closely packed together. Therefore, sound travels faster through water than through air, and even faster through steel than through water. In fact, sound travels fifteen times more swiftly through steel than through the air. Even more important than density is the elasticity of the medium. Elasticity means how well a medium can return to its initial form after being disturbed by a force. Steel has high elasticity and returns quickly to his original shape after being disturbed by a force. Cork, on the other hand, has low elasticity; rather than conducting energy, cork absorbs it.

Physical World—Answers (cont.)

6. **B. Not as high as the steel ball.** The height of the bounce of a ball is determined by the speed with which it returns to its original shape after it has been compressed on impact. This return to the original shape is what causes the ball to bounce. Rubber compresses very easily, but returns to its shape fairly slowly. On the other hand, steel compresses quickly, and returns to its shape very quickly. However, if the floor is soft, the steel ball may bounce very little or possibly not at all.

7. **B. Land on tails most of the time.** The side of the coin with "heads" on it weighs more, so over a period of time, it will tend to land on the bottom more often.

8. **A. The tip moving faster than sound.** People used to believe that the cracking sound produced by a whip was caused by the whip slapping against itself or against the air. However, Alain Goriely, a mathematics professor, proved that the sound occurs when a wave of energy travels from the handle to the end of the tip of the whip. It then snaps with such speed that it goes faster than the speed of sound and emits a small sonic boom.

9. **B. Carbon dioxide gas.** Dry ice is frozen carbon dioxide with a surface temperature of -109.3 degrees Fahrenheit (-78.5°C). As it breaks down, it becomes carbon dioxide gas, not a liquid. The fact that dry ice is extremely cold and will turn into carbon dioxide when it becomes warm makes it ideal to use as a refrigerant. Things packed in dry ice will stay frozen for a long time and will not be as messy as regular ice because there would be no water or liquid to deal with.

Name: _____ Date: _____

Rocks and Minerals

All rocks are minerals, but not all minerals are rocks. Minerals include materials that are neither animal nor vegetable. Metal ores are minerals. Crystal substances, such as salt and quartz, are minerals. Non-solids, like water and gas, are also minerals.

1. Paleolithic man used finely ground iron oxide as:
   A. Rouge.   B. Spice.   C. A cure for baldness. D. A magic potion.

2. The lead in lead pencils is made from:
   A. Pure lead.   B. Lead filings.   C. Graphite.   D. Charcoal.

3. The iron kitchen utensils of Edward III were classified as:
   A. Holy relics.   B. Jewelry.
   C. Tools of torture.   D. Instruments of worship.

4. Raw iron, the result of smelting iron ore with coke and limestone in a blast furnace, is called:
   A. Pig iron.   B. Stage one iron.   C. Iron cakes.   D. Iron maiden.

5. Of all the metals, which could humans not live without?
   A. Iron   B. Gold   C. Silver   D. Steel

6. About 300 B.C., the Chinese developed something that enabled them to defeat the Mongolians. What was it?
   A. Gunpowder   B. The stirrup   C. Bronze crossbow   D. The Great Wall

7. The only metal that is a liquid at room temperature is:
   A. Copper.   B. Titanium.   C. Uranium.   D. Mercury.

8. The term "mad as a hatter" means that a person acts as if they are insane. The phrase originated because those who made hats developed symptoms similar to those who are insane. We now know that these symptoms were caused by working with this material:
   A. Glue.   B. Mercury.   C. Cocaine.   D. Iron filings.

9. A lump of pure gold the size of a matchbox can be flattened into a sheet the size of a:
   A. Coffee table. B. 9' x 12' rug.   C. Tennis court.   D. Football field.

10. An ounce of gold can be stretched into a wire:
    A. 1 mile long. B. 10 miles long.   C. 30 miles long.   D. 50 miles long.

11. Amethyst is a variety of quartz that varies from violet to purple in color. It is considered a semi-precious gemstone. The name *amethyst* was taken from a Greek word meaning:
    A. Deep purple. B. Not to intoxicate. C. Love me.   D. Seawater.

12. In ancient times, most silver miners, within two or three years,:
    A. Earned enough to retire.   B. Became blind.
    C. Died.   D. Developed diabetes.

114

Rocks and Minerals—Answers

1. **A. Rouge.** A compact form of iron oxide is called **hematite**. Hematite varies in compactness and form. When it is in its most compact and hardest form, it is black and used in jewelry as a gemstone. This compact form is sometimes called kidney ore, because it is usually found in this shape. When hematite is crushed into a powder, it becomes red.

2. **C. Graphite.** Lead is a gray, soft metal that humans have used for thousands of years. Throughout the ages, many useful products have been made from lead. Ancient Greeks and Romans used a sharpened hunk of lead to mark papyrus, which is an early kind of a paper. While the lead made a line on papyrus, it was not very dark. Another disadvantage of using lead is that it is poisonous to humans. The ancient Greeks and Romans became aware of this when it was observed that those working in lead mines died within a couple of years. So instead of working the mines themselves, they had slaves work the mines. In the sixteenth century, shepherds discovered graphite, which they thought was lead. They called it "black lead" and used it to mark their sheep. Graphite turned out to be a good alternative to lead as a writing device. It was not poisonous and made a dry, dark mark. One problem that had to be overcome was the softness of graphite, so something was needed to hold it. People wrapped graphite with string so it would not break; eventually, wooden casings were designed to hold the graphite. The pencils we use today still have graphite inside a wooden casing. However, we *still* call the dark core inside the pencil "lead" even though it is graphite.

3. **B. Jewelry.** In the fourteenth century, iron was so rare that some iron kitchen utensils owned by Edward III were classified as jewelry. Items made of iron were items frequently stolen by thieves and robbers.

4. **A. Pig iron.** The iron maiden was an instrument of torture used during medieval times. It was a large, hinged box shaped like a human body. It was lined with spikes that, as the box was closed, pierced the victim. Iron Maiden is also a heavy metal band from London.

5. **A. Iron.** Iron is a mineral essential for life. It is found in every living cell and is important for the production of hemoglobin, an important ingredient of red blood cells. Iron helps blood and muscles deliver oxygen to every body cell; it removes carbon dioxide, as well. Iron is important for a strong immune system, mental alertness, and energy.

6. **C. Bronze crossbow.** The Mongolians were using long bows that did not shoot arrows as far or as strong as the bronze crossbow. The Great Wall was built to protect China from northern nomads. It was built over several centuries but did not protect China as efficiently as hoped. Historians believe that gunpowder was first discovered in China sometime during the Sui and Tang dynasties (A.D. 600–900) in China. The original recipe for gunpowder was not very powerful—it was basically a firecracker. It was put inside bamboo tubes and thrown into a fire. The bang would scare animals and people. The Chinese were able to make gunpowder more powerful over time and were using it for military purposes by the tenth century.

7. **D. Mercury.** Mercury is a metal, often called quicksilver, used in thermometers, barometers, electrical devices, batteries, and fluorescent lamps. Mercury is a liquid, but it is very heavy. Bowling balls, bricks, and cannonballs will all float in mercury.

115

Rocks and Minerals—Answers (cont.)

8. **B. Mercury.** The term *mad* can mean "angry" or "insane." In the case of "mad as a hatter," the term *mad* means "insane." You may be familiar with the character called the Mad Hatter in Lewis Carroll's famous children's book *Alice in Wonderland.* You may have thought that this was just an unusual character that Carroll invented. While he did create this character, the phrase "mad as a hatter" was a common phrase in 1865, when Lewis Carroll wrote *Alice.* During this time, people who made hats were called hatters, and they often seemed to go insane. They developed "hatter's shakes," which was severe jerking of the arms and legs and other muscular twitching. They also slurred their speech, had distorted vision, and some even had delusions and hallucinations. Today we know that these people were not insane but had mercury poisoning caused by exposure to mercury fumes. Mercury was brushed onto hats as they were being made. Mercury metal vapor affects the human brain, spinal cord, kidneys, and eyes. It may cause loss of memory, mood changes, problems with concentration, shaking, and other problems. Since it was the mercury vapors that caused the problems, those who bought and wore the hats did not become "mad."

9. **C. Tennis court.** Pure gold is so soft that it can be molded with the hands.

10. **D. 50 miles long.**

11. **B. Not to intoxicate.** Because of the name, people once thought that drinking wine from an amethyst cup would prevent drunkenness. It was also thought that amethyst was a cure for headaches and toothaches; would protect against disease; would protect soldiers; would make a person sleep better; and make a person smarter. The aquamarine is another semiprecious stone. Its name is taken from the Latin word meaning *seawater.*

12. **C. Died.** Silver ore was easy to find in ancient times. However, there was one big problem in mining it—rocks that contained silver also contained lead, which is poisonous. So when people mined and worked silver, they were also mining and working lead. Consequently, those who worked in silver and lead mines died of lead poisoning within a few years. In the early 1900s, in a silver mine in Canada, a lump of silver ore was found that was 100 feet long and 60 feet deep. People called it the "silver sidewalk."

Name: _____ Date: _____

 # Scientific Mysteries

Directions: Try to figure out these mysteries. Use the Internet, an encyclopedia, your common sense, or other resource materials to help you. Write the answers on your own paper.

1. Why are 75 percent of all pencils painted yellow?
2. Greg Washington, who owned a construction company, bet his sister Gail, who was a park ranger, lunch that he would see more robins over the next week than she would. Greg easily won. When Gail came to pick up Greg and take him to lunch, she waited while he tore up an old driveway. She suddenly realized why Greg had won. How did Greg win?
3. Each year, the earth weighs about 100,000 pounds more. Why?
4. A train doesn't tip over when it goes around a curve. Why?
5. When you put a conch shell to your ear, you hear a sound like waves. Why is that?
6. There is a flower called the scarlet pimpernel that is sometimes called the poor man's weatherglass. Why?
7. One man bet another that he was able to put a regular-sized apple into a bottle without cutting the bottle or the apple. He was able to win the bet. How?
8. Levi Hutchins of Concord, New Hampshire, invented the first alarm clock in 1787. It only rang at 4 a.m. Why?
9. Scientists believe there is a reason that eggs are thick on one end and narrow on the other. What is it?
10. A man visited the barber, had his hair cut short, and got a shave. That afternoon, he went camping. As the sun was setting on the first night of his trip, a blizzard began, so the man found shelter in an abandoned cabin. At sunrise, he was able to begin his journey back home. Five hours later, he walked in the door of his home. His wife noticed that he had a beard over an inch long and that the hair on his head was long and shaggy. How could this be?
11. Is it is harder on an airplane's wheels when it takes off or when it lands?
12. When high-speed trains pass each other, they slow down. Why?
13. Manhole covers are always round. Why?
14. Oak trees are struck more often by lightning than any other tree. Why?
15. It is impossible to pick a banana off the tree and then eat it. Why?
16. The Japanese have always complained that it was difficult to fit watermelons into their refrigerators because of the round shape. The watermelons would also roll around when the people tried to cut them. So the farmers solved the problem by growing watermelons shaped like a cube. How did they do this?
17. What do the following vegetables have in common? Cucumber, eggplant, pumpkin, squash, tomato, gherkin, and okra.
18. What does a baby have more of than an adult?
19. What do the following insects have in common? Firefly, wireworms, Eastern-eyed click beetle grubs, and ladybugs.
20. If it takes ten frogs ten minutes to eat ten flies, how many frogs would it take to eat 100 flies in 100 minutes?

Name: _____ Date: _____

Logic Problem: Geologists

Kendra Wilcox is taking courses to become a geologist. A geologist studies how the earth began, how it changed, and the elements that make up the earth. Kendra has just received her schedule for the next semester and discovers she is registered for five classes. Each class meets at a different time. The times the classes meet are 9 A.M., 10 A.M., 11 A.M., 12 P.M., and 1 P.M. Each class meets on a different day of the week (Monday through Friday). Use the clues given below in order to match each day with the course in which she is enrolled and the time the class meets.

CLUES:

1. Mineralogy and Chemistry are two of Kendra's most difficult classes. One meets on Monday, and the other meets on Friday.
2. The Fossils class is two days before the Hydrology class. The Hydrology class starts two hours later than the Chemistry class.
3. The class on Mineralogy begins at 10 A.M.
4. The 12 P.M and 1 P.M. classes meet on consecutive days, in some order.
5. One of the classes is Field Methods.
6. The 11 A.M. class is on Monday.

	Mineralogy	Hydrology	Fossils	Chemistry	Field Methods	9:00 A.M.	10:00 A.M.	11:00 A.M.	12:00 P.M.	1:00 P.M.
Monday										
Tuesday										
Wednesday										
Thursday										
Friday										
9:00 A.M.										
10:00 A.M.										
11:00 A.M.										
12:00 P.M.										
1:00 P.M.										

Logic Problem: Frog-Jumping Contest

Palmyra, a town near Hannibal, Missouri, decided to have a frog-jumping contest in honor of Hannibal native, Mark Twain (Samuel L. Clemens), who wrote the story "The Celebrated Jumping Frog of Calaveras County." The first year there were eight contestants. From the information given below, can you determine in which order the contestants finished?

CLUES: Billy finished sixth. Tom Thumb finished fourth. Tom Thumb finished after Blunderbuss but before Big Bertha. Big Bertha finished before Goliath but after Billy. Blunderbuss finished after Baby Dave but before Bully. Candy finished two places after Bully. List the order in which each contestant finished.

1. _____
2. _____
3. _____
4. _____
5. _____
6. _____
7. _____
8. _____

Logic Problem—Zoo Animals

The zoo in Morristown is unusual. All of the buildings are round with the cages next to the outer wall. Visitors can view the different kinds of animal by walking in a circle and then enjoy the fountains and landscaping in the center of the building. The aviary, which is the building that keeps the birds, has eight cages. On the illustration shown, the cages are labeled A, B, C, etc. Read the clues given below and see if you can discover in which cage each group of birds is located.

CLUES:

1. Going counterclockwise from the penguins, which are in cage A, to the owls, a visitor will pass the eagles and exactly two other cages in some order.
2. The shortest path from the hawks to the flamingoes passes the owls and one other cage.
3. The eagles—immediately counterclockwise from the cranes—are directly across the building from the flamingoes.
4. The storks aren't directly across the building from the cranes.
5. One cage has ostriches.

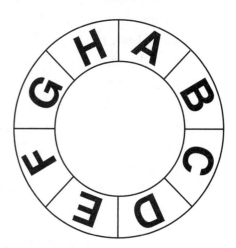

Logic Problem: The Fish Market

There is a fish market called the Great Atlantic Fish Market. All kinds of fish and other seafood is available in the store. When entering the market, the customer can see six coolers filled with seafood. The coolers are numbered 1 to 6. The numbering begins at the entrance. In other words, cooler 1 is closest to the entrance, and cooler 6 is the cooler farthest from the entrance. The shrimp is next to the scallops, and it is not the first item the customer will see when entering the market. He or she will see the salmon cooler before the sea bass cooler. Scrod are two coolers before the scallops, and the salmon is four coolers after the one with red snapper.

List the items and the order of the coolers.

1. _____
2. _____
3. _____
4. _____
5. _____
6. _____

Name: _____ Date: _____

Logic Problem: Shopping for Tropical Fish

Four friends went to a pet shop where each purchased a different tropical fish. The price of each fish was a different amount. Read the clues below, and discover each person's first name, last name, the type of fish purchased, and the price of each fish.

CLUES:

1. Brenden's fish cost less than the fish bought by the person whose last name was Butler, but more than the one who bought the molly.
2. The swordtail fish cost less than Valerie's fish but more than Fry's fish.
3. Savannah (who is not named Cole) and the person who bought the angelfish are both saving their money for another fish purchase.
4. Both Christian and the one whose last name is Fry bought some special fish food with their fish purchases.
5. "It's only money," said the girl who bought the angelfish—the most expensive fish—when Butler expressed concern about the prices.
6. The person who bought the betta (who is not Savannah) paid less than the one whose last name is Easton.
7. Both Cole, who bought the molly, and Fry will put their fish in their bedrooms.

	FRY	BUTLER	EASTON	COLE	ANGELFISH	MOLLY	BETTA	SWORDTAIL	$2.00	$2.50	$4.00	$7.00
CHRISTIAN												
SAVANNAH												
VALERIE												
BRENDEN												
$2.00												
$2.50												
$4.00												
$7.00												
ANGELFISH												
MOLLY												
BETTA												
SWORDTAIL												

FIRST NAME	LAST NAME	FISH	PRICE

Answer Keys

Science Trivia: True or False? (pg. 1)

1. False. Until the early 1960s, *spider web filaments* were used in gun sights.
2. False. Spiders are not insects. All insects must have three pairs of legs and three body segments. Spiders have eight legs and two body segments.
3. True.
4. True. Some frogs have strange calls. The wood frog quacks like a duck. The eastern narrow-mouthed toad bleats like a newborn lamb. The carpenter frog sounds like a carpenter hitting a nail with a steel hammer. The Mexican tree frog sounds like a car having trouble starting. The Mexican burrowing toad's call sounds like someone shouting "Whoa!"
5. False. A geoduck is a large clam.
6. False. Only the *male* canary sings.
7. True.
8. True.
9. True. They carried the bubonic plague which resulted in the death of one-third of the population of Europe in the fourteenth century.
10. True. A large swarm of desert locusts can consume 3,000 tons of green plants each day.
11. False. The Neanderthal's brain was *bigger* than yours is.
12. True. Different kinds of termites have various methods of defending themselves. A Nasutitermes termite soldier has a special gland in its head. This gland makes a kind of glue that it squirts out of its elongated snout. The glue tangles up the enemy so the termite is able to escape. Another termite, the African Macrotermes, forces a waxlike mixture into its attacker. The termite is also able to put a solution on an attacking ant that prevents the ant's blood from clotting. Then when the termite bites the ant, the ant bleeds to death.
13. True.
14. True.
15. True.
16. False. The *male* seahorse stores its babies inside its stomach.
17. False. A giant squid's eyes are the largest of any animal. Their eyes are bigger than dinner plates. One reason their eyes are so big is that they are huge animals. A giant squid can weigh as much as 1,980 pounds! Scientists don't know for sure where the giant squid lives, but they think it might live between 660 and 2,300 feet below the ocean's surface. With such little light available at that depth, the squid needs large eyes in order to see.
18. True. Jellyfish are an entire animal colony composed of several types of tentacles. Some tentacles take care of balance, others sting enemies, some catch prey, and others are in charge of breeding.
19. True. The liver is the only body organ that can grow back. Even if more than half of a person's liver is removed, it can grow back to its normal size in just a few weeks. If a person has 75 percent of his liver, 80 percent of his intestines, one lung, one kidney, his spleen, and his stomach removed, he can still survive.
20. False. A rainbow is not an arc, but a complete circle. Usually a person can just see a part of it. It is possible to see the whole circle when flying over clouds with the sun above you. Rainbows can also occur at night. Sometimes there are double rainbows.
21. False. The sound one hears when someone cracks his knuckles is caused by nitrogen gas bubbles bursting.
22. True.
23. True. Coconut water has been used as a substitute for blood plasma because it is sterile, readily accepted by the body, and does not destroy red blood cells.
24. False. Natural gas has no odor, color, or taste. A chemical that smells like rotten eggs is added to give it an unpleasant odor. This way, people will notice if there is a leak.
25. True. Without gravity, astronauts suffer many physical changes when in space. They get taller and their red blood cells increase. Their muscles get smaller and so does their bone density. Initially, their hearts enlarge and then shrink. It takes a while for them to return to normal when they come back to Earth.
26. False. The funny bone is a nerve and not a bone.
27. True. Want to see something surprising about our food supply? Go to http://www.fda.gov/ora/compliance_ref/cpg/cpgfod/. These are the policy guidelines and limits for what the Food and Drug Administration will allow in certain foods. For example:

Ground cinnamon: cannot contain an average of 400 or more insect fragments or an average of 11 or more rodent hairs per 50 grams of cinnamon.

Chocolate: cannot contain an average of 60 or more insect fragments per 100 grams of chocolate.

Peanut butter: cannot contain an average of 30 or more insect fragments per 100 grams; or the peanut butter cannot contain an average of 1 or more rodent hairs per 100 grams.

Cherries: Brined, fresh, canned, or frozen maraschino cherries cannot contain an average of 5% or more cherry pieces that were rejected due to maggots. The cherries cannot contain an average of 4% or more rejects due to insects other than maggots.

28. True.
29. False. Only one mile away.

The Name is the Same (pg. 8–9)

1. Bowie
2. Braille
3. Monkey wrench
4. Camel (Camel's-hair brush)
5. Barbie
6. Geiger
7. Guillotine
8. Ferris
9. Gatling
10. Diesel
11. Pasteurization
12. Sandwich
13. Colt
14. Bunsen
15. Richter
16. Mason
17. Heimlich
18. Saxophone
19. Bikini
20. Shrapnel
21. Zeppelin
22. Uzi
23. Franklin
24. Napoleon
25. Cardigan

Leonardo da Vinci Puzzle (pg. 10)
"Poor is the pupil who does not surpass his master."

Fish Idioms (pg. 27)
1. Swims very well
2. An awkward situation
3. Very crowded
4. Drinks a lot
5. An unimportant topic put in a story to take the attention away from the original issue. In a mystery, a clue might be given so the reader suspects an innocent character rather than the guilty one.
6. Hoping for a compliment
7. A person who lends money at an extremely high rate of interest
8. To have something better to do
9. A person who doesn't fit in
10. A person has other choices
11. Trying to take advantage of a confused situation
12. A very good time
13. Hard to catch or hold on to
14. Very happy

Collective Nouns for Birds (pg. 40)
1. Gulls - Colony
2. Jays - Party
3. Crows - Murder
4. Cranes - Herd
5. Eagles - Convocation
6. Hawks - Cast
7. Finches - Charm
8. Larks - Exaltation
9. Herons - Siege
10. Parrots - Company
11. Owls - Parliament
12. Peacocks - Ostentation
13. Penguins - Colony
14. Ravens - Unkindness
15. Woodpeckers - Descent
16. Woodcocks - Fall
17. Waterfowl - Plump
18. Storks - Mustering
19. Sparrows - Host
20. Turkeys - Rafter
21. Buzzards - Wake
22. Cormorants - Gulp
23. Nightingales - Watch
24. Turtledoves - Pitying
25. Coots - Cover
26. Lapwings - Deceit
27. Swans - Bank
28. Starlings - Murmuration

Find the Birds (pg. 48)
1. The book of kn**owl**edge can be read by anyone.
2. Apologies are important, thoug**h awk**ward.
3. Hipp**os prey** on unsuspecting swimmers.
4. My dog is a b**eagle**.
5. I am **raven**ous after that diet.
6. The child was given a bal**loon** for her birthday.
7. **Goo se**eped out of the bag.
8. Listen to the birds **coo t**onight.
9. I do not **regret** my statement.
10. For breakfast, he enjoyed a **flaming o**melet.
11. The keys are eit**her on** the table or counter.
12. If you will hand me the scal**pel, I can** operate.
13. When she wore her jewelry, she felt very **swan**ky.
14. Turn on the lan**tern**, so that I can see.
15. **Mac aw**akened suddenly.
16. Hand me the **wren**ch, Bob.
17. Grif**fin ch**armed his enemies.
18. C**lark** s**lowly** turned to see his attacker.
19. This is **my na**tive land.
20. Did you see these new mic**ro bin**oculars?
21. The girl and boy bo**th rush**ed to the ocean.

22. Don't be so **gull**ible.
23. Ancient humans mad**e mu**d huts to live in.
24. Would you like to s**ki wi**th me?
25. I am not poor; I am alm**ost rich**.
26. She played **a uk**ulele.
27. The emperor had a golden **crow**n.
28. When you want to come in, **buzz ard**ently.
29. The man **crane**d his neck to watch his brot**her on** the stage
30. New York is an Eas**tern** city.
31. San Francis**co, Ot**tawa, and Santiago are all cities in the Americas.
32. "I **do, do**, do," shouted the bride.
33. Laminating your ID makes your **card inal**terably safe.
34. When I was a child, I read the gos**pel. I can** read it again.

Hidden Insects (pg. 74)
1. I have always **bee**n a happy person.
2. "I **can't** find the **bug**gy," the **moth**er complained.
3. I o**we evil** men a lot of money.
4. The mam**moth** was a prehistoric creature.
5. She stopped here brie**fly** on her way to the store.
6. The swimmer was caught in the Cay**man tid**e.
7. At the end of the **term, ite**mize what you have learned.
8. The class **was p**repared for the tornado drill.
9. The holy man held the cha**lice** for all to see.
10. The girl in the pink b**louse** played a beautiful tune on her **bug**le.
11. He was the best o**f lea**ders.
12. Beware of the booby t**rap hid**den on the trail.
13. Their soccer team was the best amon**g nat**ions.
14. Warr**ant**ies can always **be e**xtended.
15. "You may app**roach** the bench," the judge said.

What's the Difference? (pg. 74)
1. **Turtle—Tortoise:** Turtles have webbed feet and live in the water. A tortoise is a turtle that lives on land. It has a high domed shell. Tortoises do not have webbed feet. Their feet are round and stumpy, making it easier for the tortoises to walk on land.
2. **Alligator—Crocodile:** Alligators are found in the southern United States and in eastern China. Crocodiles are found in Mexico, Central America, South America, Africa, Australia, and Southeast Asia. An alligator's teeth and crocodile's teeth are different. The fourth tooth on the lower jaw of a crocodile sticks up over its upper lip. The tooth is visible when the crocodile's mouth is closed. The same fourth tooth in alligators is covered. Also, crocodiles have long, pointed, V-shaped snouts. Alligators have wide, U-shaped, rounded snouts.
3. **Butterfly—Moth:** There are some differences, both physical and in lifestyle, between the two, but the most obvious difference is that most moths tend to fly mainly at night, while butterflies are active during the day.

Ants Are Everywhere (pg. 83)
1. Antarctica
2. Antennae
3. Antelope
4. Antique
5. Antlers
6. Abundant
7. Gigantic
8. Arrogant
9. Assistant
10. Lubricant
11. Plant
12. Elephant

13. Infant
14. Atlantic
15. Brilliant
16. Want
17. Chant
18. Immigrant
19. Pants
20. Jubilant

Amazing Insect Fact (pg. 91)

1. Goliath beetle
2. cicadas
3. head, thorax, abdomen
4. pupal
5. entomologist
6. prehistoric dragonfly
7. fairies
8. termites
9. caterpillars
10. proboscis
11. army ants
12. monarch butterfly
13. rhinoceros beetle
14. bees
15. cricket
16. cocoon
17. metamorphosis
18. Coleoptera
19. exoskeleton
20. ocean
21. mosquito
22. moths/butterflies
23. yellow
24. aphids
25. workers
26. ants

Fact: It was once a custom in Europe to release a cockroach into a new home.

Puzzle: "The Year There Was No Summer" (pg. 104)
Eighteen Hundred and Froze to Death

Scientific Mysteries (pg. 117)

1. During the 1800s, the best graphite in the world came from China. In China, the color yellow is associated with royalty and respect. American pencil manufacturers decided that, by painting their pencils bright yellow, it would reveal to buyers that the graphite came from China.
2. When Greg would tear up driveways and sidewalks, worms and grubs would be revealed on the surface of the ground. Robins would then come to eat them.
3. The earth is continually being showered with meteoric debris, mainly space dust.
4. The outside rail of the curve is higher than the inner rail.
5. It is the echo of the blood pulsing in your own ear.
6. If the flower is closed up, rain is coming; if it is opened up, the day will be sunny.
7. He tied the bottle to an apple tree and then put a small apple in the bottle. The fruit grew and developed inside the bottle.
8. That's what time he got up.
9. An oval or round egg would roll in a straight line. Since eggs are larger on one end, they roll in a circle. If the eggs are laid in a narrow location or on a cliff, they are less likely to roll off.
10. The man lived in a cabin very far north in Alaska. Where he lives, the sun sets in November. Alaska's sun does not rise in December or January—it rises again in February.
11. When the plane is loaded with fuel at takeoff, it is heavier when it is taking off. Consequently, it is harder on the wheels. In addition, takeoffs are faster than landings. This makes it harder on the wheels as well.
12. As high-speed trains pass each other, they produce a low-pressure area between them. The pressure is so great, it may shatter the trains' windows or pull the glass out of the frames.
13. The cover rests on a lip that is smaller than the cover. This makes it impossible for the manhole cover to drop through the opening. A manhole cover of any other shape would fall through.
14. They are usually taller than other trees.
15. Bananas have to be picked green and then ripened. If not, bacteria and insects will attack the banana on the tree as it ripens, and the banana will rot.
16. They grew the melons in glass boxes. As the watermelon grew, it took on the shape of the box.
17. They are not vegetables, they are fruits.
18. When a baby is born, he or she has 350 bones. As he or she gets older, some of these bones fuse together. An adult only has 206 bones.
19. All are beetles or beetle grubs.
20. 10

Logic Problem: Geologists (pg. 118)
Since Monday's course meets at 11:00 A.M. (clue 6), and the Mineralogy class meets at 10:00 A.M. (clue 3), Chemistry must meet on Monday, and, therefore, Mineralogy must meet on Friday (clue 1). Fossils class meets two days before the Hydrology class, and it does not meet on Monday, so it must meet on Tuesday, and Hydrology must meet on Thursday (clue 2). This leaves Wednesday for the Field Methods class to meet. The Hydrology class meets at 1 P.M. (clue 2). Therefore, the 12 P.M. class is Field Methods (clue 4). This leaves the Fossils class to begin at 9 A.M.

In summary:
Monday, Chemistry, 11:00 A.M.
Tuesday, Fossils, 9 A.M.
Wednesday, Field Methods, 12 P.M.
Thursday, Hydrology, 1 P.M.
Friday, Mineralogy, 10:00 A.M.

Logic Problem: Frog-Jumping Contest (pg. 118)

1. Baby Dave
2. Blunderbuss
3. Bully
4. Tom Thumb
5. Candy
6. Billy
7. Big Bertha
8. Goliath

Logic Problem: Zoo Animals (pg. 119)
Penguins are in cage A, the owls are in cage E, and the eagles must be in either F, G, or H. (clue 1). The cranes must either be in G or H, and the eagles must be in F or G; the flamingoes must be B, C, or D. (clue 3). However, since the flamingoes are directly across from the eagles, they cannot be B. They must be C or D (clue 3), because the eagles are either F or G. Since flamingoes are either C or D, hawks must be F or G (clue 2), but they cannot be G because the eagles are immediately counterclockwise from the cranes, so hawks must be F (clue 3). This would make the cranes in cage H, and the eagles in cage G. Flamingoes are in cage C (clue 3). Since the storks aren't directly across the building from the cranes, they must be in cage B. This leaves the ostriches to be housed in cage D.

In summary:

A. Penguins
B. Storks
C. Flamingoes
D. Ostriches
E. Owls
F. Hawks
G. Eagles
H. Cranes

Logic Problem: The Fish Market (pg. 119)
1. Red snapper
2. Scrod
3. Shrimp
4. Scallops
5. Salmon
6. Sea Bass

Logic Problem: Shopping for Tropical Fish (pg. 120)
Cole bought the molly (clue 7). Fry is not Valerie (clue 2) or Christian (clue 4). Fry's fish is not a swordtail (clue 2) or molly (clue 7), so Fry's is either an angelfish or a betta. Savannah's fish is not an angelfish (clue 3) or betta (clue 6), so Savannah is not Fry; Brenden is. Since Savannah's fish is not an angelfish (clue 3), and a girl bought the angelfish (clue 5), then Valerie bought the angelfish. The angelfish cost $7.00 (clue 5). Brenden's fish was not $7.00, $2.00 (clue 1), or $4.00 (clue 2), so it was $2.50. The molly cost $2.00 (clue 1). The swordtail did not cost $2.50 or $7.00 (clue 2), so it cost $4.00. Valerie's fish cost $7.00 (clue 2), so she bought the angelfish (clue 5). The betta did not cost $7.00 (clue 6), so it cost $2.50, and the angelfish cost $7.00. Butler's fish did not cost $2.00 (clue 1) or $7.00 (clue 5), so it cost $4.00. Easton's fish did not cost $2.00 (clue 6), so it cost $7.00, and, by elimination, Cole's fish cost $2.00. Savannah is not Cole (clue 3), so she is Butler, and by elimination, Christian is Cole.

In Summary:
Christian Cole, molly, $2.00
Savannah Butler, swordtail $4.00
Valerie Easton, angelfish, $7.00
Brenden Fry, betta, $2.50